FINDING BREATHING ROOM

ESSAYS ON MEDITATING AND LIVING

BOOK ONE

UNDERSTANDING WHY WE PRACTICE

D. M. DuMars

DEDICATION

Just as all the Buddhas of the past

Have brought forth the awakened mind,

And in the precepts of the Bodhisattvas

Step-by-step abode and trained,

Likewise, for the benefit of beings,

I will bring to birth the awakened mind,

And in those precepts, step-by-step,

I will abide and train myself.[1]

---

[1] Shantideva, Padmakara Translation Group (2008). *The Way of the Bodhisattva*, pp. 83-84. Shambhala Publications

Pause for a moment.

Notice the breath moving in and out.

Nothing needs to change.

Just this.

Foreword

If you could give yourself the freshest gift ever - fresher than a peach in August - what comes to mind?

Actually, forget the mind. Though a scholar of sorts - formally schooled in education and deep philosophy on contemplative counseling - here, our author extends a gentle invitation to the freshness of now.

A year into the pandemic, Mark and Gini DuMars called in at the UU fellowship I served at the time. Seekers who had explored spiritual paths most of their lives, they hoped to find in Tamworth, New Hampshire the groundedness of community, meaningful conversations, and a place to contribute, large or small. Their search would yield ripple effects!

A newly certified meditation instructor and a natural communicator, Mark had knowledge and experience to share. But how to do that, given the silent meditation sessions our sanctuary offered? We formed a small working group to consider the program. We gave it a name, the Tamworth Meditation Group, and a focus on outreach. So began Mark's weekly blog, *Breathing Room*. He and I consulted every Monday - he with new content, I the occasional edit - the purpose "to offer information, resources, teachings and opinions on and around the practice of meditation in our lovely little community of Tamworth, NH."

A hundred and twenty posts later, these sampling offers colorful observations on meditating and life. Open to any page and you'll find Mark in the doorway, hand outstretched in welcome: "These books are for seekers."

Mark is a devoted teacher with a knack for the written word. Moreover, his enthusiasm and curiosity brings the aliveness of meditation home. I feel and hear the snap of coarse leaves in a field of cornstalks; a bracing wind on the face, kids on a mountainside; images that remain - a fly on a window, sunrise in the Smokies. The lucid brilliance of masters ever deep and fresh.

"We're here to experience life as only humans can," says Mark. "This might enhance your life." Curious? Come on in.

Rev. Elizabeth M. Tabor
February 2026

Mt Chocorua, Tamworth, New Hampshire

INTRODUCTION

"The secret of your future is hidden in your daily routine."
<u>Mike Murdock</u>

Here we are. We have finally arrived at the scary, unimaginable place we dreamed of as kids: THE FUTURE! To many of us, our arrival seems a culmination of lives well lived. People, places, and things coalesced. To others, things happened so fast we felt unprepared, but we are still upright, breathing, owlishly gazing.

And to a few, we continue to be in complete denial of inevitability. Some of us are strong and steady whereas others may have health concerns and are living lives of constant worry and grief. Some of us seem financially secure where others do not.

And yet, here we are. We are still breathing in and out. Are we curious about that? Have we been paying attention to life as it unfolds? For some of us, we have been able to keep pace with the details, foresee possible outcomes and plan accordingly.

For some, life zigged and zagged unpredictably and it seemed that it was hard to stop and catch our breath. And for some, we seemed overwhelmed from the beginning and only through sheer resilience did we arrive here and now.

Whatever timeframe we are experiencing in this lifetime, how do we want to see it play out? What tools do we have in place to observe its progress? Do we become afraid and hide, do we ignore it altogether or do we embrace its inevitability? How are we dealing with the day to day right now? Are we constantly so overwhelmed with thoughts and emotions that we don't notice the raindrops on the window? Are we having trouble sleeping? Or can we simply be here-and-now observing each day as if it's brand new? What gets in the way? As each day comes and goes, these might be important questions.

There is a saying out there in the world: "How we do anything is how we do everything." So, two reasonable questions at this time of our lives could be, "*What are we doing* and *who are we being* in this moment?" What comes up for us as we even consider these two questions?

Although my life has certainly had its ups and downs, I make no claims of having "arrived" somewhere significant as a result. My experience of life so far has fallen somewhere in the bell-curve of "normal" in that I am still here and still seem to have the wherewithal to be thinking things in my seventh decade.

Along the way I have read a few books and picked up a few tools offered by some very smart people that might be helpful to at least, retain some dignity as I notice body parts sagging toward the floor.

Just for background around where I'm coming from, as a child, my life just was what it was. Looking back as an adult, it would be easy to blame my early poor self-esteem and the problems I created on my parents, on circumstances, on the Navy, on alcohol or drugs, or on luck.

To be frank, I was born with some intelligence, little common sense, and few clear examples to follow. Because of that lack of common sense, I had poor judgement when it came to decision making. I lived from a reactive state to anything and everything. The results somehow reinforced my negative self-perception which was smothered by an ego that wanted to be seen. I had no clue that this was even a thing until I entered sobriety at 33 years old. Even then, old habits, behaviors and a huge imposter syndrome seemed to dominate my perception.

It took quite a while for that to settle, while trying to be authentic and avoid as many pitfalls as I could.

I don't see my progression as exceptional. It was made up of what I personally experienced and how I dealt with it at the time. Everyone reading this has had their own experiences, some good, some not and some not remembered. Deepak Chopra, an enlightened Internal Medicine physician and spiritual teacher alluded to this individuality using the metaphor of waves in the ocean. Each wave is as distinctly unique as a fingerprint. There are no identical waves, yet they all arise from and fall back to the same source.

Personally, after years of trying to make sense of my experience, I finally realized that it was what it was, and I would not be who I am or have the awareness that I do without having gone through all that. I found that reflecting on the past had been somewhat helpful, especially if I could stand back and observe those memories through the lens of who I *was* at the time. I was a completely different person when I was 5 or 14 or 20 or 40 years old and my world view was limited by what I had experienced up to that point. Comparing what I know now to what was seen then has opened compassion around what that kid or person went through. He just didn't know any better at the time.

Most often though, the memories were shadowed by *subjective* emotion. These many years later, those emotions have often become indelible and concrete. They appear to have reinforced the interpretation of each experience whether it was actually true or not. It became difficult to be objective and see the actual lesson.

Neuroscience states that the brain does not know the difference between what it remembers and what it is currently experiencing. I found myself habitually re-living my memories as if they were happening right now. Except they were seen through the lens of who I was at the time of the occurrence. They were overwhelming and too disorganized by black-and-white thinking, cause-and-effect, or reward-punishment, or emotions like guilt, resentment, victimization, or blame. This all came to a head when I found myself being revived on an emergency room table.

Looking back, it seems that the only way my attention could be captured long enough to actually learn something about myself was for the Universe to "slap me in the head with a two by four" (figuratively). The remarkable thing I noticed as I regained consciousness was the *silence*. I had been so accustomed to the almost demonic negative self-talk that the following silence seemed profound. I didn't know what to do other than try to wrap it around me so I could rest. I realize now that I had been experiencing some kind of self-imposed, *subjective* trauma response.

I am not sure that you, as the reader, can relate to what was just written, but if put into a diagnostic context, the words trauma, anxiety, depression, and overwhelm may feel familiar. *Subjective* means viewing from an individual's singular experience and is colored by opinions, biases, and reactive states. *Objective*, on the other hand, means a general, agreed-upon description. This experience of silence reminded me that my mind was incapable of forgetting, but it also demonstrated that there was a possibility of coming to terms with the past without overwhelming the present. I needed to think about things differently.

I began what became a decades-long study and search for meaning through many different venues from Christianity to Islam, Hinduism to Buddhism, New Age to Nativism. What I found was much the same instruction and ideology wrapped in different structured packages. It was slow going at first, because I would tend to skim and absorb, but what I saw was fascinating and beautiful.

I found that world history was rich in teachings, methods, protocols, and first-hand experiences written about for over 5,000 years. However, reading and studying did not reveal the silence I was seeking. It was many years before I realized that what I had glossed over was the *one key* requirement that could offer a step-by-step approach through this labyrinth called life. That key requirement suggested that I somehow establish a simple discipline that could help me find enough peace to begin looking over my current and historical experience *objectively*.

I was eventually introduced to the practice of meditation. I was told it could become a discipline that could eventually offer me the silence I sought. I found wonderful videos, recordings and podcasts available that offer teaching from basic, fundamental practices to advanced techniques.

These were incredibly informative, but they all had one thing in common: they required some form of external device and/or subscription to see, hear, and experience them. Many suggested postures, environments, tools, clothing, or sound to employ their practices. They eventually did not work for me because I would become attached to their *processes*. Unless I was wearing some kind of "new age" clothing, had a player or TV, I just could not do it on my own. I needed to embody a practice to understand it.

At 62 I retired from my previous work and went back to graduate school to segue into clinical mental health counseling. I had realized that sitting around in "retirement" was not my cup of tea. The school I chose, however, helped me kill two birds with one stone. I could achieve licensure through their program, but their program *required* me to meditate 7 – 10 hours a week and had two-week required silent retreats every semester. To me, it was kind of like a "boot-camp" approach to philosophy and meditation. I knew that my biggest weakness was distraction. Left on my own, I would procrastinate, fiddle around, and never develop a discipline. But, if they required the practice, I could override my own sketchy impulses.

The school was Naropa University in Boulder, Colorado, and the program emphasis was Contemplative Buddhist Psychology. It was created by Chogyam Trungpa Rinpoche back in the late seventies as a way to introduce Buddhist philosophy through Psychology. The primary tool to achieve this was a Tibetan meditative form called Shamita Vipassana (peaceful abiding), and one didn't have to become Buddhist to graduate from the program.

Something I really liked was, though the training was rigorous, it trained the students to meditate anywhere from noisy airports to the deep woods. There were no attachments or accoutrements. The practice could be unceremonious or rigid depending on the likes or dislikes of the practitioner, but there was strong emphasis on non-attachment which to me meant no internal or external requirements to practice. For the first time in many decades, I began to again experience silence. It was in me all along.

D. M. DuMars
Spring, 2026

Contents

PART ONE

WHY WE SEEK

"So, what is a good meditator? The one who meditates"

Allan Lokos

Meditation reduces stress and anxiety in general.

There are many ways to meditate. At last count, over 3,000 forms have been named, all with the same goal in mind: To help teach us ways to bypass the noise of our conscious mind and rest.

That mind, as incredibly important as it is, is really just a fascinating tool to help us understand our experience. Unfortunately, most of us were not taught to see it that way and assume that what goes on "up there" in the brain must all be true…because it's in our brain.

A scientific study from the *University of Wisconsin-Madison* indicates that one form of meditation, the practice of "Open Monitoring Meditation" (such as Vipassana), reduces the grey-matter density in areas of the brain related to anxiety and stress.

In other words, less density equals less overwhelm and anxiety. Meditators were more able to essentially "watch" the stream of thought without getting stuck on any one of the 50,000 thoughts we all experience every day.[2]

---

[2] Sources: NCBI, Wiley Online Library, The American Journal of Psychiatry, ScienceDirect, American Psychological Association, American Psychosomatic Medicine Journal, Medical News Today

MYTHS AND MISCONCEPTIONS

"Feelings come and go like clouds in a windy sky. Conscious breathing is my anchor."
Thich Nat Han

1) "It takes years to get any benefit"

Research shows that meditation brings great physical and mental health benefits after even as little as 8 weeks of practice.

Meditation produces many levels of benefit. If you want to attain enlightenment, or be in a fearless state beyond all suffering, then yes, it will require a bit of patience. But if all you want is better health, a bit more peace and balance in your life, you can start having that in a few weeks.

Another way of looking is that meditation's benefits are immediate. Practice itself is the benefit. You will usually feel better after all your meditation sessions – more relaxed, more focused, more rested. And it's free; all it costs is your attention.

2) "Meditation is escapism/running away from problems"

Anyone that has done meditation for a decent length of time knows that it's the other way around. Meditation makes all the stuff that you are trying to run away from – in your life and in yourself – painfully clear.

Everything you try to escape from is right there, in your mind, waiting for you. It's actually harder to escape our own shadows once we are in meditation. That is actually the reason some people find meditation so hard, especially in the beginning: all the not-so-pretty stuff we're hiding or ignoring comes to the surface.

On the other hand, it is true that some people do try to use meditation to avoid looking at their problems. Once they get skilled enough in the practice, they are able to bring their attention to a peaceful place, inside their consciousness, which is beyond all problems. Meditation simply gives them a tool to control their mind and attention; what they do with it is their choice.

Meditation helps you to know yourself, to see things more clearly and to control your mind. If you use this "power" to turn the blind eye on things that need real action outside yourself, don't blame it on the practice.

Conclusion: meditation will not make you run away from your problems... It will take you to a place that is deeper than them. From there you will emerge with the needed clarity and resources to meet them skillfully, if you so wish.[3]

---

[3] **Adapted** FROM: Published at: http://liveanddare.com/myths-about-meditation

UNMET EXPECTATIONS

"To accept some idea of truth without experiencing it is like a painting of a cake on paper which you cannot eat."
Suzuki Roshi

Thich Nhat Hahn said,

"Bhikkhus (students), the teaching is merely a vehicle to describe the truth. Don't mistake it for the truth itself. A finger pointing at the moon is not the moon. The finger is needed to know where to look for the moon, but if you mistake the finger for the moon itself, you will never know the real moon. The teaching is like a raft that carries you to the other shore. The raft is needed, but the raft is not the other shore. An intelligent person would not carry the raft around on his head after making it across to the other shore. Bhikkhus, my teaching is the raft which can help you cross to the other shore beyond birth and death. Use the raft to cross to the other shore, but don't hang onto it as your property. Do not become caught in the teaching. You must be able to let it go"[4]

Many folks find that when they begin considering a practice of meditation, they already have preconceived notions and expectations around what that means. Maybe they have read a little about it, or maybe they heard someone like Deepak Chopra mention it.

Possibly, they ask their friends about their experiences which may seem either good or bad. Maybe they participated in an American Yoga class and were told that THIS is meditation. All in all, people form an impression before they actually experience it, and based on that impression, choose to participate or not; choose to become curious or not.

My personal experience, before learning from real teachers, was artfully colored by my "know-everything" mind, much like the cake Suzuki Roshi describes above. I *thought* I knew the truth around what

---

[4] FROM: https://ideapod.com/25-profound-zen-buddhism-quotes-on-letting-go-and-experiencing-true-freedom-and-happiness/

meditation *was*, having spent the better part of the preceding two decades studying, reading, interviewing, feeling energies; doing absolutely anything other than setting a meditation discipline.

In other words, my mind was full to the brim with knowledge, but no practice. I was "All hat and no cowboy." Even when I finally did sit for my formal teachings, my mind was so full of thoughts and conflicting emotions that I actually could not hear what was being taught until I learned one simple trick – sit down and watch your breath… don't make it do anything, just watch it come in and go out.

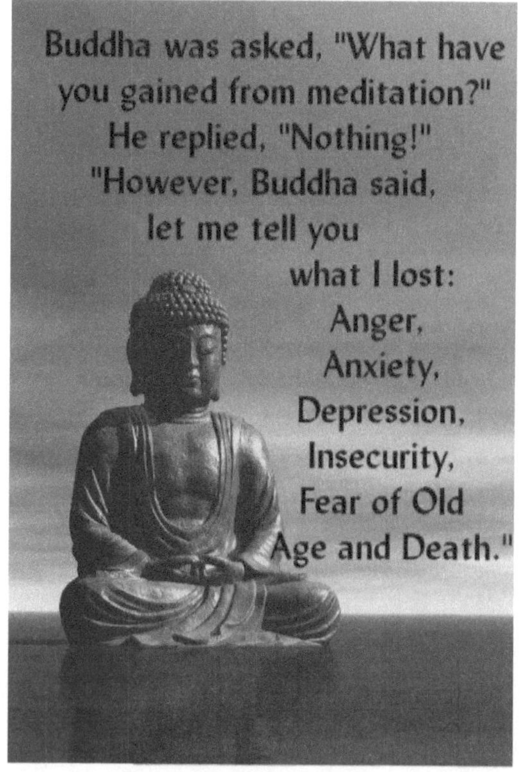

MEDITATION REDUCES THE RISK OF HEART DISEASE AND STROKE

"If you have time to breathe, you have time to meditate. You breathe when you walk. You breathe when you stand. You breathe when you lie down"
Ajahn Amaro

More people die of heart diseases in the world than any other illness. In a study published in late 2012, a group of over 200 high-risk individuals was asked to either take a health education class promoting better diet and exercise or take a class on Transcendental Meditation.

During the next 5 years researchers accompanying the participants found that those who took the meditation class had a 48% reduction in their overall risk of heart attack, stroke, and death. They noted that meditation "significantly reduced risk for mortality, myocardial infarction, and stroke in coronary heart disease patients.

These changes were associated with lower blood pressure and psychosocial stress factors."

WHAT MEDITATION IS – AND ISN'T (PART ONE)[5]

"The aim of meditation is to transform the mind. It does not have to be associated with any particular religion. Every one of us have a mind and every one of us can work on it."

Matthieu Ricard

This section draws on teachings by Matthieu Ricard, as presented in *Meditation: A Practical Guide to Making Friends with Your Mind* and related published teachings.

In our modern world, we are often carried from one activity to the next, rarely pausing long enough to notice the deeper causes of our happiness or dissatisfaction. Even with access to comfort and convenience, many of us continue to feel a quiet sense of restlessness.

Meditation offers a way to begin seeing this more clearly—not by adding something new, but by gently observing the patterns already in place.

But no change can occur if we simply allow our habitual tendencies and automatic patterns of thought to perpetuate and even reinforce themselves, thought after thought, day after day, year after year. Those tendencies and patterns can be challenged…this is where meditation comes in. Its aim is to transform the mind.

"Meditation is a practice that makes it possible to cultivate and develop certain basic positive human qualities in the same way as other forms of training make it possible to play a musical instrument or acquire any other skill… meditation helps us familiarize ourselves with a clear and accurate way of seeing things and cultivate wholesome qualities that remain dormant within us unless we make an effort to draw them out…we [tend to] wander about in confusion like a beggar who is simultaneously rich and poor because he does not

---

know he has a treasure buried under his hut… the goal of meditation, specifically, is not to shut down the mind or anesthetize it, but to make it free, lucid and balanced."

In our modern world, we are often carried from one activity to the next, rarely pausing long enough to notice the deeper causes of our happiness or dissatisfaction. Even with access to comfort and convenience, many of us continue to feel a quiet sense of restlessness.

Meditation offers a way to begin seeing this more clearly—not by adding something new, but by gently observing the patterns already in place.

This is not about becoming something different.

It is about seeing what is already here—clearly, directly, and without the need to immediately change it.

WHAT MEDITATION IS – AND ISNT (PART TWO)[6]

'By breaking down our sense of self-importance, all we lose is a parasite that has long infected our minds. What we gain in return is freedom, openness of mind, spontaneity, simplicity, altruism: all qualities inherent in happiness.'
Matthieu Ricard

"Meditations … are based on the experience of generations of meditators who have devoted their lives to observing the automatic, mechanical patterns of thought and the nature of consciousness. They then taught empirical methods for developing mental clarity, alertness, inner freedom, altruistic love, and compassion.

However, we cannot merely rely on their words to free ourselves from suffering. We must discover for ourselves the value of these methods these wise people taught and confirm for ourselves the conclusions they reached. This process requires determination, enthusiasm, perseverance, and what the 8th-century monk and scholar Shantideva called "joy in virtuous ways."

Thus, we begin by observing and understanding how thoughts multiply by association with each other and create a whole world of emotions, of joy and suffering. Then we penetrate the screen of thoughts and glimpse the fundamental component of consciousness: the primal cognitive faculty from which all thoughts arise.

If we consider that the potential benefit of meditation is to give us a new experience of the world each moment of our lives, then it doesn't seem excessive to spend at least twenty minutes a day getting to know our mind better and training it toward this kind of openness.

The fruition of meditation could be described as an optimal way of being, or as genuine happiness. This true and lasting happiness

---

[6] By **Mathieu Ricard** IN *Meditation Made Simple/Practices for a Happier Life*, Lions Roar, Special Eds. Fall, 2023, pp 12-15, excerpted for brevity

is a profound sense of having realized to the utmost the potential we have within us for wisdom and accomplishment. Working toward this fulfillment is an adventure worth embarking on."

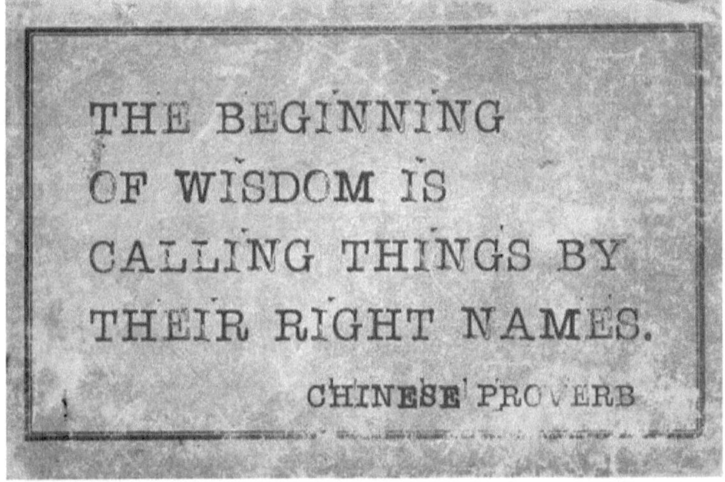

"Self-observation is the first step of inner unfolding."
Amit Ray

It seems that, as we go through our lives, our attention is nearly always focused outwardly on people, places, things, events, or emerging experiences. The rest of the time, we focus on the past and how we remember things, often defining ourselves by those memories. So, it is unusual in our culture to look at the mechanizations of our own minds. What goes on in our own minds is mostly seen as true, unaltered, and objective.

Meditation is a somewhat unusual practice in our culture, though it is gaining popularity among those who feel there must be "something else" beyond what we are experiencing. And, as with some of the popular New Age methods, where participants are led through imagined experiences, it can be tempting to abdicate any personal responsibility around observing themselves and simply follow the instructor's lead.

When they practice this at home, unless they record it beforehand, they find "meditating" can be difficult and uncomfortable as there is no one outside of themselves to tell them what to do. With all due respect to the instructors, there often isn't time to introduce the participants to introspection when there is an hour or two-hour curriculum that must be completed.

This can also be analogous to the various religions we encounter where the sermons or teachings are part of an agenda meant to invite a self-reflective practice but does not include time to experientially show the participants the nuts-and-bolts that set the foundation of that practice.

This is where fundamental meditation practices come in. They have been taught and refined for over 7,000 years and prove that meditation is a practice leading to a strong and refined self-discipline. It is as simple as that.

Discipline is defined as:
 a) control gained by enforcing obedience or order
 b) orderly or prescribed conduct or pattern of behavior -or-
 c) SELF-CONTROL [7]

The key term here is "self-control." We are all familiar with this concept when it applies to our outward behavior, but, outside of engineering, mathematics, or science, we were NOT taught that our minds must become disciplined too or they can stray into awkward, uncomfortable places and take up residence there. Many of us were not taught that we have options when it comes to the thoughts in our heads.

Fundamental meditation is grounded in the FACT that we can observe our own thought processes. Most of us already do this before sleep. Some of us are able to actually dismiss those processes and go to sleep right away. This is a discipline we have practiced over time.

Fundamental meditation teaches us to extend that discipline to dismiss those thought processes AT WILL and remain alert at the same time. The benefit? Being able to sort through the normal cacophony and find the peace that the discipline "floats" in. Otherwise, that peace remains elusive to most of us when it is "hidden in plain sight."

---

[7] https://www.merriam-webster.com/dictionary/discipline

BECOMING QUIET

"The quieter you become the more you are able to hear."
Rumi

Two thousand, five hundred years ago, after his experiences with the reality of life outside of the privileged bubble he was born into, it is said that Gautama Siddhartha found enlightenment and a solution to suffering through six years of intense meditation and self-reflection. He was thirty-three years old. He then spent the next fifty years writing and teaching about his experience so that others may find the same answers that he did. He taught that the release of suffering could be heard in the heart if the mind could become quite enough to hear it. Few understood what he was trying to teach, but some of the population was curious and ready to listen to what he had to say. His teachings remain today.

Two thousand years ago, it is said that another being, Jesus of Nazareth was born into poverty and a different culture that had an intrinsically rigid belief system in place. We know little about his early life, but when he was thirty years old, he also began sharing his own experiences of "the kingdom within" and began teaching others about prayer, meditation and conduct so that they might find the same answers he did. He also taught that the release of suffering could be heard in the heart if the mind could become quite enough to hear it. Few understood what he was trying to teach, but some of the population was curious and ready to listen to what he had to say. Unfortunately, some of the people thought that his teachings were too radical and undermined their rigid authority. They conspired and, when he was thirty-three, had him crucified. His teachings also remain today.

If nothing else, these two simplified examples underline that if one can quiet the mind, profound personal understandings around the nature of life begin to arise from the heart. Both individuals instructed that the mind, a wonderful tool to navigate this terrestrial experience, was simply that, and that it had no place in the deeper, unfolding awareness we all experience when we can get it quiet for a minute.

Through quieting the mind and listening, we tune in to something quite profound; quite beautiful and complete. Eckhart Tolle said,

> *"When you become aware of silence, immediately there is that state of inner still alertness. You are present. You have stepped out of thousands of years of collective human conditioning."*

Meditation gently introduces us to what we can experience when we quiet our mind. We can tune into some of the beautiful and unexpected understandings of why we are here.

"If we commit ourselves to staying right where we are, then our experience becomes very vivid. Things become very clear when there is nowhere to escape."
Pema Chödrön[8]

I personally draw on many of the Buddhist teachings because of their inherent pragmatism around how to handle experience. It's true that there have been over 33 different points of view (complete religions) around the meaning of Gautama Siddhartha's teachings, just as there have been many diverse religions taken from the teachings of Jesus of Nazareth and Mohammed. They too offered beautiful, pragmatic approaches to this thing called "life" but included more existential teachings around the nature of God and Man in the process.

After his enlightenment, Siddhartha ("Buddha" means "awakened one"), contrary to his Hindu heritage, avoided the metaphysical, focusing instead on "mindfulness." According to the sutras (teachings), he emphasized focusing on the here-and-now experience and disciplining the mind to become aware of the change/impermanence offered within each moment.

"To live on this shifting ground, one first needs to stop obsessing about what has happened before and what might happen later. One needs to be more vitally conscious of what is happening now. This does not deny the reality of past and future. It is about embarking on a new relationship with the impermanence and temporality of life. Instead of hankering after the past and speculating about the future, one sees the present as the fruit of what has been and the germ of what will be. Gotama did not encourage withdrawal to a timeless, mystical now, but

---

8 Pema Chödrön, When Things Fall Apart: Heart Advice for Difficult Times, Shambhala, 1996

*an unflinching encounter with the contingent world as it unravels mo-
ment to moment."*[9]

We practice. Although we meditate together, we are supporting one another in strengthening a discipline that helps us to remain "in our seat" regardless of outside stimulus or internal thought patterns evident in each moment. Remarkably, we have all experienced a difference in how we handle impermanence compared to how we were before joining a group.

---

[9] Stephen Batchelor IN https://bigthink.com/thinking/buddhist-wisdom/

"Meditation is interacting with truth inside and scientific research is interacting with truth outside. Both are required for human evolution, emancipation and empowerment"
Amit Ray[10]

Up until now, the focus of this book has explored the lived experience of meditation—why we practice, how we begin, and what unfolds over time. Much of this has been personal and experiential.

Here, we turn briefly toward what scientific research suggests about meditation and its effects on the mind and body. Some may quietly wonder what research has to say about all of this.

I am drawing in part on the work of Ritchie Davidson and Daniel Goldman in, *Altered Traits: Science Reveals How Meditation Changes Your Mind, Brain, and Body* (Avery, 2017) which examines decades of research into the long-term effects of contemplative practice.

As reported by Alvin Powell in the Harvard Gazette, researchers have explored how mindfulness-based practices may influence mental health:

> "Many people don't respond to the frontline interventions… Individual cognitive behavioral therapy is helpful for many people; antidepressant medications help many people. But it's also the case that many people don't benefit from them as well. There's a great need for alternative approaches …." - Benjamin Shapero, Harvard Medical School

Shapero is working with Gaëlle Desbordes, an instructor in radiology at HMS and a neuroscientist at MGH's Martinos Center for Biomedical Imaging, to explore one alternative approach: mindfulness-based meditation. ….

Powell notes that studies have shown benefits against an array of conditions both physical and mental, including irritable bowel syn-

---

[10] Amit Ray, IN Compassionate Artificial Intelligence (2018)

drome, fibromyalgia, psoriasis, anxiety, depression, and post-traumatic stress disorder."[11]

Much of the early research on meditation focused on "state" effects - how meditation influenced attention, mood, performance in the moment. Some studies were limited in scope or design, while others offered reliable findings. When we begin to look more closely, especially at long-term practitioners, a clearer picture starts to emerge. One of the most consistent findings is the strengthening of attention itself.

In one study, participants who completed an eight-week mindfulness program demonstrated a significantly improved ability to sustain attention compared to those who had not undergone the training.

Not all the research was that rigorous, and some turned out to be little more than hype. But when you weed out the studies that don't meet the highest scientific standards, as Goleman and Davidson have done in their book, a clear picture emerges of what we know about the science of meditation—and what we still need to learn.

Not surprisingly, some of the strongest areas of research center on attention. In one key MIT study, researchers found that volunteers who took an eight-week Mindfulness-Based Stress Reduction program had a far greater ability to focus on their sensations than a control group that hadn't done the training.

Another study at the University of Wisconsin showed that only 10 minutes of breath-counting helped offset the damaging effects on concentration of heavy-duty multitasking.

Still another study, from the University of California, Santa Barbara, revealed that merely eight minutes of mindfulness practice improved concentration and reduced mind-wandering.

The researchers also found that mindfulness had a dramatic effect on working memory—the facility we have to manipulate stored information in order to reason and make decisions in a timely manner.

---

[11] https://news.harvard.edu/gazette/story/2018/04/harvard-researchers-study-how-mindfulness-may-change-the-brain-in-depressed-patients BY Alvin Powell, April 9, 2018

One group of students that underwent a two-week course in mindfulness training boosted their scores on their GREs—the graduate school entrance exams—by more than 30%.[12]

THE SCIENCE OF MEDITATION – PART TWO

"The discovery of truth by slow, progressive meditation is talent. Intuition of the truth, not preceded by perceptible meditation, is genius"

Johann Kaspar Lavater[13]

This article is "part 2" introducing some of the double-blind, placebo-controlled experiments conducted to study the effects of meditation. Certainly, this list is not exhaustive as some very fascinating research is being conducted all around the world at this point. The information herein is simply a "taste" to demonstrate that mindfulness meditation, cliché aside, is being taken very seriously in the upper echelons of academia as the "next" viable evidence-based healing modality. The biggest challenge and biggest threat to the AMA and psychological community is how to monetize it.

Researcher Gaelle Desbordes is probing mindfulness meditation's effect on depression, using functional magnetic resonance imaging (fMRI) to take before and after images of the brains of depressed patients who've learned to meditate. The work seeks to understand the internal brain processes affected by mindfulness meditation training in this population.

Desbordes' interest in the topic stems from personal experience. She began meditating as a graduate student in computational neuroscience at Boston University, seeking respite from the stress and frustration of academic life. Her experience convinced her that something real was happening to her and prompted her to study the subject more closely, in hopes of shedding enough light to underpin therapy that might help others.

"My own interest comes from having practiced those [meditation techniques] and found them beneficial, personally. Then, being a sci-

---

[13] Aphorism 93 (1787), in *Aphorisms on Man.* Translated from the original manuscript of the Rev. John Caspar Lavater (3rd ed. 1790), 36.

entist, asking 'How does this work? What is this doing to me?' and wanting to understand the mechanisms to see if it can help others," Desbordes said. "If we want that to become a therapy or something offered in the community, we need to demonstrate [its benefits] scientifically.

Desbordes is part of a community of researchers at Harvard and its affiliated institutions that in recent decades has been teasing out whether and how meditation works.

Other MGH researchers also are studying the effects of meditation on the body, including Sara Lazar, who in 2012 used fMRI to show that the brains of subjects thickened after an eight-week meditation course.

Work is ongoing at MGH's Benson-Henry Institute; at HMS and Brigham and Women's Hospital's Osher Center for Integrative Medicine; at the Harvard-affiliated Cambridge Health Alliance, where Zev Schuman-Olivier directs the Center for Mindfulness and Compassion; and among a group of nearly a dozen investigators at Harvard and other Northeastern institutions, including Desbordes and Lazar, who are collaborating through the Mindfulness Research Collaborative.

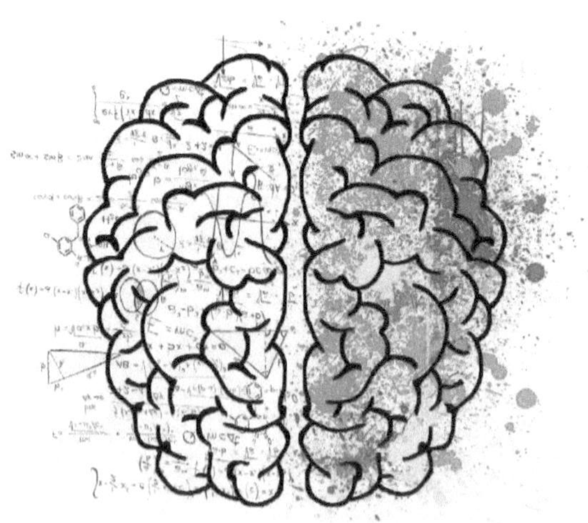

THE COCOON

"I feel that our permanent condition is akin to being in a little tent in the Himalayas late at night. We may have a lantern or a flashlight, but otherwise we're surrounded by the vast darkness of the nighttime sky, pinpricked with stars. We're surrounded by things far greater and larger than we are, and how ready we are to accept them will define how happy our lives will be."[14]

Pico Iyer

In the article from which the above quote is taken, Pico Iyer, an author of fifteen books on contemplative travel, goes on to suggest that it's only when we're at home and in our heads that we assume we're so different from others. He suggests that travel in any form takes us out of our preconceived notions and dumps us into a reality which is always much more grand and complex than what we think it is. He goes on to describe how our 19th century, preconceived, isolationist view of the world is completely upended when we go to Boston, New York, or any other metropolitan city. How we think things *should* be doesn't fit into a hugely expanded, multicultural environment. If we are not scrambling to escape that, we have no choice but to be humbled into the recognition of the very real collective interdependence that makes up the rest of the world.

Chogyam Trungpa Rinpoche, a Tibetan Buddhist teacher describes a cocoon that we all construct to protect that precious "Me" inside it. There is "Me," then there is everything else. It is what we hold up to separate us from perceived reality and reality itself. He said,

"In the cocoon, there is no idea of light at all, until we experience some longing for openness, some longing for something other than the smell of our own sweat. When we examine that comfortable darkness - look at it, smell it, feel it - we find it is claustrophobic. Then, we realize

---

[14] Pico Iyer, July 25, 2023, IN https://www.lionsroar.com/pico-iyer-travel/?goal=0_1988e44b2-e8d000993c-27317280

Mindfulness meditation is a form of traveling. With practice, we can release our preconceived notions, habits, and thoughts to do what they will while we simply observe their nature. It is the same with travel. We go somewhere that is alien to our daily cocoon and we have no choice but to experience the expansion of our awareness.

"Mindfulness is like a microscope; it is neither an offensive nor defensive weapon in relation to the germs we observe through it. The function of the microscope is just to clearly present what is there."

For a moment, as our cocoon falls away, we can sit in wonder at how large our world really is.

---

[15] https://www.quotetab.com/quote/by-chogyam-trungpa/mindfulness-is-like-a-microscope-it-is-neither-an-offensive-nor-defensive-weapon

STRUGGLING WITH MONKEY MIND?

"Stop leaping from wave to wave, looking for water"

-Anon

Do any of these experiences sound familiar?[16]

Restlessness   Stress & tension   Insecurity   Irritability & re-activity
Negative self-talk   Low energy levels   Fear   Poor sleep
Self-doubt   Regrets   Emotional Eating   Procrastination

If so, you may be suffering from the dreaded *Monkey-Mind*. It is an ancient Buddhist concept that describes a state of restlessness, capriciousness, and lack of control in one's thoughts and seems to have originated from Chinese xīnyuán or Sino-Japanese *shin'en* 心猿, a word that literally means "heart-mind monkey." (Wikipedia) It also is an incredible adaptation our minds have had to make in order to process the sheer volume of daily data they have to take in here in the 21st Century.

Our minds are literally biological AI systems. From birth, they are *programmed* to take in data from our five senses, compare it to our base programming (*see Maslow's Hierarchy*), overlay it with our past experience and produce decision-points moving forward.

There seems to be irony in the fact that we all *see* our minds doing this stuff. It can feel like watching a movie unfolding inside our head. We end up with either clogged *"data-redundancy"* or a filter system that has become so concrete that we actually stop processing data and simply rely on our memory – which changes, by the way, based on the contextual experience one is having while trying to remember.

---

[16] FROM: https://liveanddare.com

Because it's going on in our head and most of us can *literally see* it, we assume that all we are seeing is real and true when neuroscience has proven that what we are *seeing*, is actually a matrix of randomly fired electrical particles connecting our brain cells which we interpret as *thoughts*.

Experts estimate that the mind thinks between 60,000 – 80,000 thoughts a day. That's an average of 2500 – 3,300 thoughts per hour.[17] Then there is *"overflow."*

Our brains do not shut off at night. When we have cut off most of the other senses by lying down to sleep, the brain has nothing else to do but continue processing. If we are experiencing these many thoughts in a 24-hour period and we DO NOT have some sort of discipline to filter, organize or drop these thoughts, we end up with Monkey-Mind.

This is where meditation comes in. In a gentle sequence of practices, one learns to disengage with that flow of thought for a little while. It's like giving the brain a break for a moment so it can catch its "breath."

One learns to establish a discipline that is useful in all walks of life, not just on the cushion. As our friend Ed Parson's says, "We learn to get slow." Oh, yes, the brain does continue to frantically process huge amounts of data, but that's its job. In meditation, we're just learning not to micro-manage as much.

[17] source: https://www.successconsciousness.com/

GETTING HOOKED

"You can actually feel shenpa happening. It's a sensation that you can easily recognize. Even a spot on your new sweater can take you there. Someone looks at us in a certain way, or we hear a certain song, or walk into a certain room, and boom—we're hooked. It's a quality of experience that's not easy to describe but that everyone knows well."

Pema Chödrön[18]

As this is being written, a grand, early Spring snowstorm is hitting this region of New Hampshire. The fact is, at this moment there is snow falling from the sky. That's it. That's all there is to it. I see little birds huddled and fluffed in the pine branches. The quiet is tangible as is the cold. The car appears to be buried.

As I write, I notice that it is so easy to get "hooked" and carried off into all sorts of directions and descriptions and metaphors and judgements about a snowstorm when the point of this piece is to introduce "*shenpa*." Shenpa is a Tibetan word that means "hooked" or "attached." What I am experiencing is just another example of how my mind can take ANY form of stimulus and turn it into a narrative that I then internally or externally react to.

> "Now, if you catch shenpa early enough, it's very workable. You can acknowledge that it's happening and abide with the experience of being triggered, the experience of urge, the experience of wanting to move. It's like experiencing the yearning to scratch an itch, and generally we find it irresistible. Nevertheless, we can practice patience with that fidgety feeling and hold our seat… in these moments, we can con-

---

tact the underlying insecurity of the human experience, the insecurity that is inherent in a changing, shifting world.

As long as we are habituated to needing something to hold on to, we will always feel this background rumble of slight unease or restlessness. We want some relief from the unease, so when shenpa arises we go on automatic pilot: without a pause, we follow the urge and get swept away…

The best way to develop our ability to stay fully present with shenpa and to equate that with lovingkindness is in meditation. This is where we can train in not getting swept away. ” - Pema Chödrön (source as above)

So, I present an invitation. When you glance at the picture below or out the window in your home, notice what comes up for you. I will do the same.

THE SELF

"Meditation is not what you think. You sit in absolute silence, and your mind starts going over all your movies. During that process, you become so familiar with the scripts you keep in your life that you end up getting sick of them. Then you realize that the person you think you are is nothing but a complicated script you spend most of your energy on.
After a more thorough examination, you discover your personality disgusts you, and that's because it's not really you. If you feel terrified enough about that personality, you spontaneously allow it to fade away. Then, if you're lucky, you can experience yourself without the distortion of that personality.
There's so much talk about the mechanics of happiness - psychiatry and pills, positive thinking, and ideology - but I really think the mechanism is there. All you have to do is get quiet for a moment."

Leonard Cohen

Ever had any curiosity around what our "self" actually IS? Where "IT" is found, or how we define it? I believe it's what we identify as "me" when we are thinking or talking to others. It's the "I" when referring to our singular view. It is a place-name holder to distinguish and separate the viewer from that that is viewed.

This is "normal," right? This is what we all feel, right? To even consider that on an energetic level there is no separation "between" all living things is ludicrous, right? And an even sillier concept would be that the Self doesn't actually exist, right?

The wonders of science and technology have explored nearly every aspect of our brains and what has become remarkable, beyond the trillions of neurons held together within a bowling ball-sized cranium, is that absolutely NO evidence of a "self" has been found. There is no "me," no "I," no sign of anything other than a lump of living, tightly packed neurons that seem to be involved in their own complicated lightening display of "random" bio-electric energy.

That energy has shown that it habituates into channeled energy based on experience, much like a Tesla coil is attracted to a local filament, except meaning is not made around the Tesla display. It's just a display for our entertainment.

On the cellular level, between the neurons, there is space. On the molecular level, there is an incredible amount of space between molecules and, on the atomic level, well, it's been said that if you blow up the nucleus of an atom to the size of a basketball, the first electron ring would be over 100 yards away. So, like sheet music, there is far more meaningful space on the page than notes that communicate what a composer wants us to feel.

As the Leonard Cohen quote above suggests, we have unlimited opportunities to "stand back" for a minute and simply watch the display. We have unlimited opportunities to "stand back" for a minute and CHOOSE to not be personally named by the interactive "movie." What would that be like? WHO would we BECOME? WHERE would we GO? HOW would we function?

I suspect that the world we take part in would become much bigger, much brighter and much more fulfilling if, for just a minute, we could be less "self" involved and allow "life" to continue around us.

Give it a try… see what you think. I think you'll be pleasantly surprised.

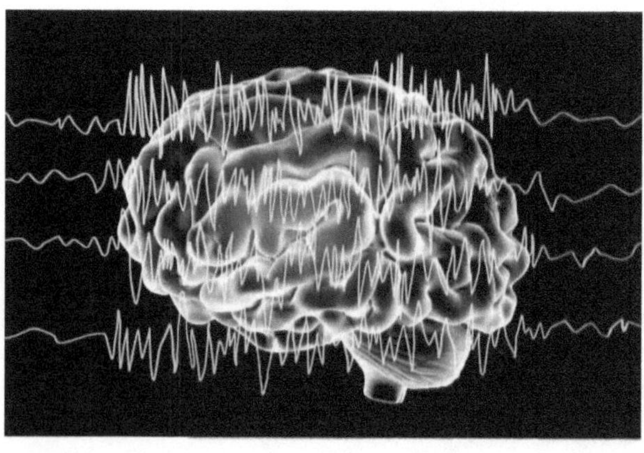

"To enjoy good health, to bring true happiness to one's family, to bring peace to all, one must first discipline and control one's own mind. If a (person) can control (their) mind (they) can find the way to Enlightenment, and all wisdom and virtue will naturally come to (them)."

Buddha[19]

Maybe it's just me, but I sense an unease in our nation, in our communities and within ourselves. I can say, in personal observation, that my mind habitually reaches beyond itself seeking cause… and frankly, it is never disappointed. There seems to be a never-ending list of "reasons" WHY.

The other part of me, somewhat better disciplined, knows that the REAL reason for this personal discomfort is because, for the moment, I had become distracted. The following is an excerpt from an article written by one of my teachers that helps explain this phenomenon.

> "Meditation practice is not an exotic or out-of-reach approach. It is immediate and personal, and it involves an intimate relationship with ourselves. It is getting to know ourselves by examining our actual psychological process without being ashamed of it.
>
> We are often critical of ourselves to the point where we may become our own enemies. Meditation is a way of ending that quarrel by making friends with ourselves. Then we may find that we are not as bad as we thought or had been told we were.
>
> If we label ourselves as hopeless cases or see ourselves as villains, there is no way to use our own experience as a step-

---

[19] The original, 2,600-year-old text of this quote was typically gendered. This text was parenthetically updated to 21st century social justice considerations. md

ping-stone. If we take the attitude that there is something wrong with us, we must constantly look outside ourselves for something better than we are. That search can continue indefinitely on and on and on.

In contrast to that approach, meditation is contacting our actual situation, the raw and rugged state of our mind and being. No matter what is there, we should look at it. It is similar to building a long-term friendship with someone. As part of the process of becoming friends, you get to know things that you do not like about someone, and you meet parts of the relationship that are very uncomfortable.

Acknowledging the problems and coming to terms with them is often the foundation for a long-term friendship. Having included those things from the beginning, you won't be shocked by them later on. Since you know all the negative aspects, you don't have to hide from that side of the relationship. Then you can cultivate the other side, the positive side, as well.

That is also a very good way to start making friends with yourself. Otherwise, you might feel surprised and cheated later on, when you discover the things that you've been hiding from yourself.

Whatever exists in us is a natural situation. It is another dimension of natural beauty. People sometimes go to great lengths to appreciate nature by climbing mountains, going on safari to see giraffes and lions in Africa, or taking a cruise to Antarctica.

It is much simpler and more immediate to appreciate the natural beauty of ourselves. This is actually far more beautiful than exotic flora and fauna, far more fantastic, painful, colorful, and delightful."

RESPONSIBILITY

"Meditation is to be aware of every thought and of every feeling, never to say it is right or wrong, but just to watch it and move with it. In that watching, you begin to understand the whole movement of thought and feeling. And out of this awareness comes silence."

Jiddu Krishnamurti

To many of us, even to some of our leaders, the *idea* of taking an hour, or fifteen minutes, or even a moment out of our day, to just sit down and breathe while watching our thoughts is enough to induce anxiety. For some reason unbeknownst to me, many of us obsessively and compulsively support a high degree of stress, energy, focus, whatever, to our experience both in what we do and to how we think.

There seems to be a great deal of judgement around "doing nothing." And to many, meditation is "doing nothing" because there seems to be no purpose, no goal, no accomplishment, or money to be made just sitting there like a log… doing nothing.

For most of my life, I could have described my habitual thoughts and behavior as I have above. I did not know how to relax, to play, or to just momentarily step out of my waking life to just give myself a break. That was what sleep was for. Upon waking in the morning, I was like a high-rpm diesel tractor trundling along until I shut down at night. I could not lay blame elsewhere and because I saw nearly everyone else caught in the same obsessive-compulsive grind, I thought maybe it was normal and let it go.

I was programmed by self, culture, environment, maybe even survival to be constantly on the go. I was an automaton and didn't know it. It was not until I had an "out of body" episode during a near-death experience that I realized that this type of living was NOT normal. I could actually see the non-cognitive, habituated programming that had no end point.

Shockingly, I could also see what I had been missing in that tunnel-vision-life I had been living. I realized that life, in nearly all aspects, has an ebb and flow to it; that beauty and love (agape) pop up everywhere; that moving *with* life was so much more fulfilling than valiantly swimming upstream; and that so much more can be done because the previous iteration had been so inefficient.

I had been wearing out the bearings in my own hamster wheel because I was not being responsible for this incredible gift of life I had been generously afforded.

So, I sought to change things. I found that a meditation discipline is the ONLY way to become objective around the nature of our personal thoughts and actions. We actually begin to take on our deep responsibility to ourselves and others. Mindfulness requires staying in the here-and-now, objectively triaging what is right in front of us, and providing the wherewithal and skill to take a step forward.

Walking meditation is a real-world metaphor of how to do that. Sitting meditation is how to objectively study the context within which *everything* is happening *now*. The path becomes simple because the options open right in front of us. And guess what? We don't die if we give it a try.

"It turns out that our ability to connect with other people is driven by our ability to connect deeply with ourselves. And that can be just a few minutes sitting on your porch feeling the breeze against your face. That can be a few moments spent in meditation or in prayer or remembering three things you're grateful for."
Vivek Murthy

ANGER

"Mindfulness is always mindfulness OF something, just as anger is always anger AT something. When you drink a glass of water and are aware that you are drinking a glass of water, that is mindfulness of drinking water. In this case, we produce mindfulness of anger. "Breathing in, I know I am angry. Breathing out, I know that anger is in me." First the energy of anger arises, and second the energy of mindfulness arises. The second energy embraces the first in order to soothe it and allow it to subside."

Thich Nhat Hahn[20]

I'd say that over half of my life was ruled by anger. As Thich Nat Hahn alludes to in the article I referenced in the quote and endnote, I carried a "store consciousness" from early childhood that contained the seeds for almost any emotion. People, places, or things would trigger the spontaneous growth of one of those seeds and I would react explosively as if the trigger were at fault.

The most dominant seed in my "store" was anger. It was also the most dominant seed in my parent's store, so I was taught well how to nurture that seed. By the time I was in my thirties, I had burned so many bridges through that anger that there was never going to be a way "back." Maybe that was a good thing in a way. I had no choice but to move forward.

Mindfulness meditation saved what remained of my life, but it took a while before I really understood how. For so long, I unconsciously thought that anger had always been a power I could wield in order to uphold boundaries, get my needs met, maintain dominance or put people in their place. It never occurred to me that those I was angry at were suffering too and now more so because I was heaping my anger on them.

---

[20] From Teachings on Love, by Thich Nhat Hanh. © 1998. Reprinted with permission of Parallax Press, Berkeley, CA. IN https://www.lionsroar.com/mindfulness-practice-transform-anger-into-love/

I tried to spiritually offload it through religion, exercise, martial arts or by trying to deny it. It wasn't until I slowly began internally acknowledging my anger, becoming friends with it because it was a PART of me, that I began to have a little space around it.

It took a while for me to realize that, because I thought it was real, I took care of it as I would a chained pet. When I was taught mindfulness meditation, I came to the realization that I don't like chained pets; that if you simply love them as they are, they don't get out of hand.

I was taught to do what Thich Nat Han said above. *"Breathing in I know I am angry. Breathing out I know that anger is in me."* This was a radical new way of seeing the issue. I was able to become objective, relaxed and look deeper into the cause and effect.

Mindfulness meditation provided me the space to begin having compassion for myself for carrying this weight for so long. And I began to see the unconscious epigenetic generational flow, the chain of suffering throughout my family.

Mindfulness meditation has provided me the opportunity to introduce the concept to others that because we feel things it doesn't mean our lives are defined by those feelings. They are just energy spikes in the waveforms of our lives.

CHOICE

"It may not seem like it, but when you are stuck in fearful and despairing thoughts, you do have a choice. You do not need to let your thoughts and reactions run wild. You can interrupt the pattern. You can slow down enough to investigate the cascade of thoughts, speculations, opinions, and emotions aroused by hearing about all the troubles in the world."

Judith Lief[21]

I am noticing that when I wrote this issue of the Breathing Room newsletter, it's "due date" fell on an auspicious occasion nationally. It was Election Day and by the hundreds of millions, good, responsible people from all walks of life participated by casting their individual choices for "the future."

Some of them felt it their duty; some felt panicked and pressured; and some did not participate at all, succumbing to a nihilistic narrative that says whatever they chose would not matter in the long run.

But I am wondering how many of those hundreds of millions of folks consciously choose the next step in their experiences each and every day and how many feel compelled by daily pressures to reach out in their panic, like grabbing a hanging limb when caught in a flood?

The Three Poisons, as described in Buddhist liturgy, are Greed (craving or grasping), Hatred (anger or pushing away), and Delusion (ignorance). The animalistic tendencies - of grasping for what we don't have, pushing away what we don't want, or completely ignoring what the impermanence of life imposes on our experiences - are deeply ingrained and the source of ALL of our suffering and discontent. Who knew? The remedy… simply making conscious choices.

---

[21] https://www.lionsroar.com/how-not-to-freak-out/ by Judith Leaf, 3Nov2020

In black-and-white thinking, how could anyone possibly make "conscious" choices when our experience in life is like that of a grasshopper in a chicken coop – totally reactive to circumstance? When we are so overwhelmed by stress and inundated by "alt-truth" information that we don't know where to turn? When, as some Christians might say, the Lord of this world has been given a free hand to create chaos when all we really want is peace and security? With all that, what choices do we have, right?

So, sometime during your day, before you make an important choice, do yourself one simple favor: It's a nice day… Take a walk. Breathe the air. Feel the earth under your feet and ask yourself, in this moment, "Who am I?"

Keep repeating the question until no answer remains. It will take a few minutes before you run out of superficial labels, but keep going – out there, your feet in the earth, breathing the air. For a moment, just allow the cacophony in your head to dissipate, relax into the environment that you are a part of, and breathe.

Now that you are ready, make a choice.

CONFIRMATION BIAS VERSUS DIALECTICAL THINKING

"Truth is stranger than fiction, but it is because Fiction has to make sense"

Mark Twain

Confirmation bias is the tendency to search for, interpret, favor, and recall information in a way that confirms or supports one's prior beliefs or values.[22] *Dialectical thinking* involves a complex way of understanding that sees contradiction and tension between opposites as a key characteristic of all things. In other words, it is defined as discovering what is true by considering opposite theories.[23]

The practice of meditation continues to be somewhat of a conundrum. On one hand, it can be an "add-on" to our busy day. It can be a form of "something different" from our routine, or a newly imposed discipline to "make us better."

To some, it may be important how others see them, as in, "I want people to think I'm spiritual and a meditation practitioner." And to some, it can be a form of refuge where it's understood that during the time of practice, we are not disturbed by things "out there." These considerations can confirm or support one's belief around what meditation is and why it's practiced.

On the other hand, some see meditation as a method to dissolve the self or ontologically contemplate the nature of being. Theoretically, bypassing the self can open vast vistas of existence and one can begin to understand more mystical teachings taught through philosophy and religion. These considerations also can confirm one's beliefs.

So, which is it? Is meditation a practice to focus on self or to focus on not-self? Is it a method to "get our house in order" or to abandon

---

[22] https://en.wikipedia.org/wiki/Confirmation_bias

[23] https://search.brave.com/search?q=define+dialectical+thinking&source=desktop&summary=1&conversation=6ae87b20408cef48d2143b

our house altogether? I guess following the rule of confirmation bias, it would depend on who you ask.

Dialectical thinking offers something different. Confirmation bias seems to dictate a this *OR* that view. Frankly, we all seem to experience and possibly contribute to this perception. Its foundations have historically been taught in our schools, our churches, our politics and have even been found as a pillar of capitalism.

Dialectical thinking differs in that it offers a this *AND* that view. In other words, it is inclusive. Fundamentally, it sees all reality (being) as encompassing everything that is within it. It is sort of like the "sky" metaphor spoken of in "The Song of Milarepa" written by an 8th century yogi.

So, to someone open to the idea of meditation, maybe taking a wide, all-encompassing view may be more informative when considering beginning a practice. Looking at one's own opinion is valuable, but that opinion may not complete a picture. Listening to podcasts, watching videos, or following someone that wants one to think they know what they are talking about may also provide a piece of the picture. Wearing the right clothes, sitting in a new way, lighting incense and candles, humming, and listing to someone telling one what to do can, again, be part of a picture.

To get an authoritative fundamental all-encompassing knowledge, one eventually must add all that information to personal experience to complete the picture. And until that is done, does one truly know what the practice of meditation is? In other words, one needs to become curious and find out for themselves.

NOT DOING, BUT BEING?

"Meditation is not evasion; it is a serene encounter with reality"
Thich Nhat Hahn

A lot of people have commented that they "just can't sit around doing nothing" or, "if I sit still for any length of time, I go to sleep." That's because most of us have our entire lives oriented around *doing* things. We wake up in the morning and have our daily agenda at hand, sometimes before we get out of bed. Each task, whether novel or habitual, is made up of step-by-step processes. Taking a shower, brushing our teeth, getting dressed, going to work, taking a break, picking up the kids, working in the garden, meeting an appointment, all require some sort of structure so that we can begin and end before we go on to other tasks. Some of the tasks are so habituated that while we are accomplishing them, we are usually thinking of what is next or something random.

Our egos have been programmed to accommodate all the things that make up our experience. As we get older, more and more of those experiences become routine which means that WE, the observers of this life, are released from the responsibility of overseeing our egos in their processes. It's like the videos out there that show folks falling asleep while riding in their self-driving cars.

Meditation is about taking time to step out of our machine-like living structure and simply observing what's actually going on. Initially the ego rebels because it doesn't know what to *do*. If the ego doesn't know what to *do*, it becomes confused, off balance and defensive. It causes people to become impatient, grumpy, or sleepy.

As one continues to meditate, one gradually becomes aware of *being*. *Being* means that in the here-and-now, one is truly alive and observing the world through the five senses without engaging in it.

It can be like standing at the top of a tower or mountain and looking at all there is to see. Each moment brings something new into the equation to fill our perception of the present moment.

One of the first realizations new practitioners notice is just how much of *life and meaning* they have been missing as they filled their hours with constantly *doing* things. At the end of the day, they often find themselves exhausted and really can't remember what they have been *doing*. When they add a few minutes of meditation to their day, they go to sleep remembering points of beauty, poignant experiences, and a deep sense of having actually *lived* a full day.

PART TWO

ESTABLISHING PRACTICE

"The practice of meditation helps us to release the tension — within the body, within the mind, within the emotions — so that healing can take place,"

Thich Nhat Hahn

"Before you learn how to meditate, it's helpful to know what meditation is. The most common form of meditation is breath meditation, or mindfulness meditation, in which you bring your attention to your breathing.

While breathing in and out, observe when and how your mind wanders to thoughts — for example, everyday stresses of relationships and work — and then return your focus to your breath.

By learning to continually bring your attention to your breath and releasing your thoughts without judgment, you are training your consciousness to remain in the present moment. Making this a habit can lead to an emotionally stable state of mental clarity.

Healing through meditation can take many forms. There are meditation practices that help manage daily stress and anxiety. There are meditations that reduce pain; promote relaxation; and others that enhance empathy and compassion.

Other forms of meditation include the body scan, walking meditation, and loving-kindness, or *meta* meditation."[24]

With practice, meditation can help us remain stable and present in the midst of triggering or controversial experiences such as driving, shopping or political arguments. A clear and present mind offers an opportunity for one to choose a wise and grounded path when it seems that our lives are anything other than that.

---

[24] FROM https://www.Lion'sRoar.com

THE PULL

Saint Theresa, a 14th century Carmelite nun wrote in her book The Inner Castle about the powerful pull we all have toward the existential. She describes a dream where she finds herself wandering around in the dark surrounded by snakes and poisonous things, being terrified at every turn yet feeling unerringly pulled toward the center of a castle made up of seven rings or walls. Something tells her that if she can make it through, she will be free and will join with The Beloved, but initially, she doesn't even know why she feels that pull. I don't know of anyone, at some point in their life, who doesn't feel like they are supposed to be doing something important; who feels some sort of pull toward the existential; a pull beyond themselves and their experience.

So once one gets to the point in their lives where they can't resist the pull; where everywhere they turn is dissatisfaction; where nothing they do seems be the "it" that will release them from their "snakes and poisonous things" inside their heads and all around, they search outside of themselves for an answer, or a ritual, or a specialist or a drug that can save them. They find that either none of it works or they are pharmaceutically stupefied which, at least, hides the cause of their suffering. But some have heard that establishing a discipline or a practice of meditation has been proven over the centuries to be a path through the darkness. Being at wit's end, they decide to really give it a go. What have they got to lose? And nobody else seems to care anyway.

So, once they've gotten beyond the cliché, the stigma, the narratives (demons) in their head that do everything to dissuade the practice, they sit and begin. It's shaky at first, but anything is better than what chased them here; is better than the years of feeling the pull and doing nothing about it. And an interesting phenomenon begins to emerge. Although nothing "out there" has changed; people are still being jerks, politics are still wonky, the kids still never call, and the weather seems determined to get in the way, it all seems ok for now. The iron grip around unmet expectations begins to soften, and beauty previously unseen begins to emerge everywhere. Understanding begins to dawn that the source of their suffering has always been in the way that they used to see and participate in the world.

There is a story from Ancient India of six blind men led to an elephant standing in the compound. Each man touches a different part of the elephant's body (trunk, tusk, ear, leg, side, or tail) and describes it based on their limited experience. The first man, touching the trunk, says it's like a snake; the second, touching the tusk, says it's like a spear; and so on. The blind men then compare their descriptions, and each one argues that what THEY perceive is the REAL elephant and everyone else is wrong. Eventually, they begin to realize that each of their perspectives is partially correct, yet incomplete. They eventually come to understand that their individual experiences are limited and that there is more to the elephant than they can perceive.

HERE WE ARE. ARE WE HERE?

"What a liberation to realize that the 'voice in my head' is not who I am. Who am I, then? The one who sees that."

Eckhart Tolle

In a previous chapter, there was a short article about breath and how becoming aware of it and controlling it can help us relax. To reiterate, if you are reading this, you must be breathing. If you are not breathing, just skip this issue, we'll catch up on the "other side." But if you are breathing, you may find the following helpful.

Anxiety in all of its forms seems to underline nearly everything. It is an absolutely normal, natural survival reflex planted way back when our species were not the apex predators on the planet.

"In these anxious times, there are plenty of stressors affecting our breathing. Moment to moment, we may be unconsciously anticipating the next ping of our phone or the next horror in our feed. The looming chaos in our political and planetary atmospheres weighs on us constantly, along with the ever-present demands of work and family. Meanwhile, Covid has forced us all to reckon with the profoundly interdependent nature of breathing ... however, we have agency in relation to our breath. The practice of mindful breathing not only reveals that respiration is both automatic and voluntary, it empowers us to choose the quality of breath appropriate to each moment"[25]

Eckhart Tolle said, "The peace you want is already in you, you just can't feel it because the mind is making too much noise."

One way to release yourself from the onslaught is to simply be here…

---

[25] BY Melvin Escobar IN https://www.lionsroar.com/how-to-practice-mindful-breathing-for-anxiety/?goal=0_1988ee44b2-458dfbdc86-27317280 26November2024

NOW. How do we do that? Through our breath.

NOW, sit still.

NOW, take a deep breath and slowly let it go.

NOW, take in another one and let that go.

NOW, simply watch your breath as it softly flows in and out.

Did you notice something?

For that moment, you were not anxious.

For that moment, your mind was occupied with the activity.

NOW, take in another breath imagining it going out to your toes and fingers.

NOW, as you release your breath, imagine all of your tensions flowing out with it.

Try to do this five times without other thoughts crowding in.

Do it NOW.

This is not yesterday or last week or in the past, nor is it tomorrow or in the future. This is all happening NOW. This moment is the only time you are alive as you are observing your breathing and observing the habitual thoughts trying to crowd in. You are not your thoughts. You are observing them. You are not your breathing. You are observing it. You are observing, breathing, and reading… NOW.

This practice is simple and there is a 100% guarantee: If you try this simple method and you don't like it or just casually dismiss it, you get every bit of your anxiety back, no questions asked.

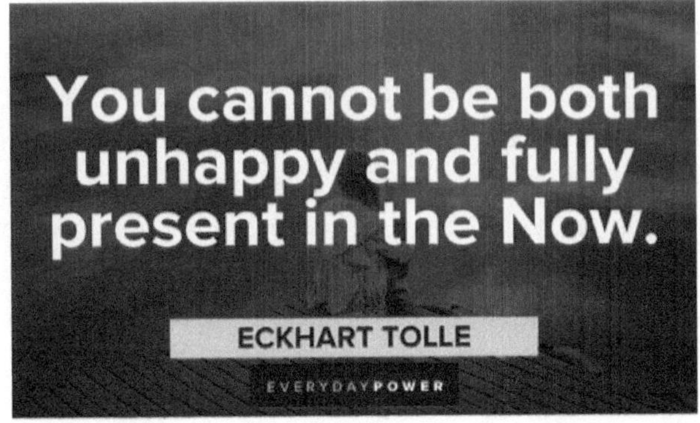

BREATHING

"When you arise in the morning, think of what a precious privilege it is to be alive, to breathe, to think, to enjoy, to love."

Marcus Aurelius

Except for those of us who have suffered breathing issues in our lives, most of us take breathing for granted. It is something that is just there whether we are awake or asleep. Most of the time, we only become aware of it when we are "out" of breath like exertion; if we pick up a virus or have a condition that affects our lungs; or are having a panic attack.

Our attention is habitually on everything else like taking out the garbage, minding the kids, feeding the animals, recreating the past, using magical thinking to predict the future, or making up new evidence to support a resentment. Breathing is just something that takes place in the background like weather or air conditioning. It just happens while we wait for our lives to unfold.

Little children breathe from their bellies naturally. I was watching my 2-year-old grandson laughing, squealing, and running from one side of the living room to the other. I noticed he never became "out" of breath and that his little tummy moved with his breathing. That is something that is emphasized in meditation instruction. A straight posture, a soft front, and breathing from the belly.

I have to admit that because of a lifetime of experiences both outside and inside of my head, I developed shallow "chest-breathing." My mind says it's because of this or that, or because I was victimized, or have constant anxiety, or because the future is really scary.

The *truth* is that I have shallow breathing because I have had a lot of practice at shallow breathing, and it has become a habit. It is the reactionary *sympathetic nervous system* response to stress, and we are constantly preparing ourselves to fight, flee, freeze, or collapse.

Perhaps we never learned that an emergency response is not supposed to be constant; it will burn us out. Or maybe we never learned that like prey animals, we need that response when we need it and we're supposed to balance it with an immediate, *parasympathetic response* when we don't. That way we survive for another day.

Meditation is all about stimulating that parasympathetic response which calms us down and returns us to normal. To do so, meditation teachers invite us to become aware of our breathing as it comes in – to our belly – and how it goes out from contracting our belly, dissipating into the air around us.

Because breathing is fundamental to life, we can count on it being there as our constant anchor. We watch our breath come in; we watch our breath go out. Simple as that.

In its most fundamental nature, meditation teaches us to be fully present with *THIS* moment and whatever is taking place within it right *NOW* anchored by our breath. Not yesterday, not tomorrow, not even in the next minute, *NOW*. We become aware that we are only alive in this moment right *NOW*… everything else is a figment of our imagination.

As a side benefit, we come to realize that there's a whole lot more going on right *NOW* than we were aware of a few minutes ago: birds singing, cool air smells, distant livestock noises, pollinators buzzing, love of another, deep compassion for the beauty in this moment, maybe even gratitude as we watch our breathing.

"Meditation should not be regarded as a learning process. It should be regarded as an experiencing process. You should not try to learn from meditation but try to feel it. Meditation is an act of nonduality. The technique you are using should not be separate from you; it is you, you are the technique. Meditator and meditation are one. There is no relationship involved"

Chogyam Trungpa Rinpoche[27]

Mind and body are interdependent. Because the state of one affects the state of the other, a correct sitting posture is emphasized for meditation. The seven-point posture, used by experienced meditators for centuries, is recommended as the best way to help gain a calm, clear state of mind.

1. Legs

If possible, sit with your legs crossed in the vajra, or full-lotus, position where each foot is placed, sole upward, on the thigh of the opposite leg. An alternative position is the half-lotus where the left foot is on the floor under the right leg and right foot on top of the left thigh. You can also sit in a simple cross-legged posture with both feet on the floor. A firm cushion under the buttocks will enable you to keep your back straight and sit longer without getting pins-and-needles in your legs and feet. If you are unable to sit on the floor in any of these positions, you can meditate in a chair or on a low, slanted bench. The important thing is to be comfortable.

2. Arms

Hold your hands loosely on your lap, about two inches below the navel, right hand on top of the left, palms upward, with the fingers aligned. Shoulders and arms should be relaxed. Your arms should not

---

[26] Adapted from: How to Meditate: A Practical Guide *by Kathleen McDonald, Wisdom Publications.*

[27] IN https://elevatesociety.com/quotes-by-chogyam-trungpa/)

be pressed against your body but held a few inches away to allow circulation of air: this helps to prevent sleepiness.

3. Back

Your back is most important. It should be straight, held relaxed and lightly upright, as if the vertebrae were a pile of coins. It might be difficult in the beginning, but in time it will become natural, and you will notice the benefits: your energy will flow more freely, you won't feel sluggish, and you will be able to sit comfortably in meditation for increasingly longer periods.

4. Eyes

New meditators often find it easier to concentrate with their eyes fully closed. This is quite acceptable. However, it is recommended that you leave your eyes slightly open to admit a little light and direct your gaze downwards. Closing your eyes may be an invitation to sluggishness, sleep, or dream-like images, all of which hinder meditation.

5. Jaw

Your jaw should be relaxed and teeth slightly apart, not clenched. Your mouth should also be relaxed, with your lips together lightly.

6. Tongue

The tip of your tongue should touch the palate just behind the upper teeth. This reduces the flow of saliva and thus the need to swallow, both of which are hindrances as your concentration increases and you sit in meditation for longer periods.

7. Head

Your neck should be bent forward a little so that your gaze is directed naturally towards the floor in front of you. If your head is held too high you may have problems with mental wandering and agitation, and if dropped too low you could experience mental heaviness or sleepiness.

This seven-point posture is most conducive to clear, unobstructed contemplation. You might find it difficult in the beginning, but it is a good idea to go through each point at the start of your session and try to maintain the correct posture for a few minutes. With familiarity it will feel more natural, and you will begin to notice its benefits.

The practice of hatha yoga or other physical disciplines can be a great help in loosening tight muscles and joints, thus enabling you to sit more comfortably. However, if you are unable to adapt to sitting cross-legged you can make a compromise between perfect posture and a relaxed state. In other words, keep your body and mind happy, comfortable, and free of tension.

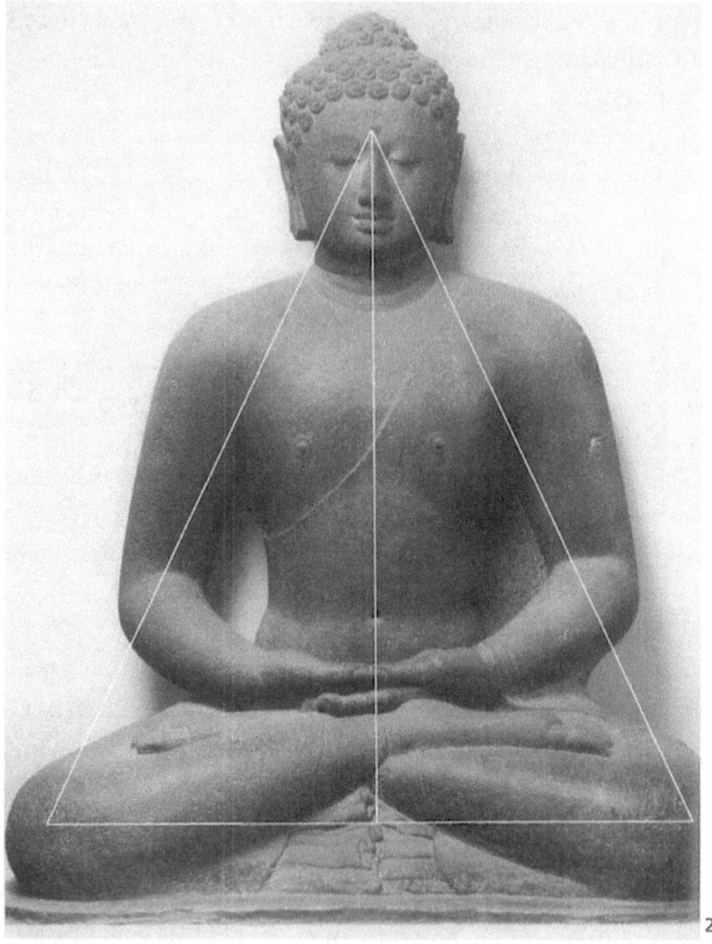

[28] Image courtesy of Museum Nasional, Jakarta

BEGINNING YOUR DAY

*"If you eat a live frog first thing in the morning, nothing worse will happen
to you the rest of the day"*

Mark Twain

As alluded to above, sometimes it's best to tackle the most difficult things in our day by getting them done right off the bat. First
thing in the morning, we have energy, we can be alert, and our patience hasn't worn thin yet, particularly when we have the habit of
judging ourselves. Many of us are "night-owls" and don't necessarily
wake up until later, but even then, we are refreshed and ready to give
it another go when we do finally get out of bed.

The teachers, gurus, and masters of the many religions that practice prayer and meditation all agree that the best time to meditate is
in the morning before the day begins. They say it's like building a
house on a solid foundation. The rest of the day would then reflect
that practice. Think of the times when we began our days grumpy,
disgruntled, depressed, lonely, angry, or tired. Wasn't our experience
of the day a reflection of how we began it?

Paramhansa Yogananda, a Hindu teacher from the 1950's suggested the best time for meditation is between 3:00 and 4:00 AM
when the rest of the world is sleeping. He also has said that one hour
of meditation is the equivalent to 4 hours of sleep. Reportedly, he
only slept for two hours a night but meditated for six. In today's
world, that practice may seem impractical, but I think that the notion
is correct.

So, first thing in the morning, have your coffee if you have to;
have your shower if that's your habit, but then… sit down, or if the
weather permits, take a walk. Don't look at the phone or the tv. Don't
start worrying.

Just listen to the birds and forest waking up. Notice the air, the
clouds, the greenery. Notice the quiet and breathe that in. Just for a

little bit, just for a moment. When it's time, when you are still feeling peaceful, end the practice and get on with your day.

Before you go to sleep, reflect on your day and see if anything has changed. I bet you'll be pleasantly surprised.

BEING A LOG

"Meditation is not just blissing out under a mango tree. It completely changes your brain and therefore changes what you are."

Mathieu Ricard

The story goes that the Buddha, while sitting on the banks of the Ganges River, observed a large log being carried along by the current. He asked his monks if they saw the log and then explained that just as the log flows effortlessly along the river, unresisting and unattached to its surroundings, a mindfulness practitioner should strive to cultivate a similar mindset. In today's national climate and particularly with the experiences of the recent past affecting everyone in some way, the idea of "being a log" may seem antithetical.

The Buddha's simile above may provide an antidote and a workable method to get past particular, painful "stuck" places we are currently finding ourselves in. Cultivating non-attachment to thoughts, emotions, and desires can allow for a sense of freedom and detachment without ignoring what is happening "out there."

Through mindful awareness, we can acknowledge the present moment and what is arising right in front of us while still being aware of our surroundings. The log's journey is shaped by the river's currents and eddies, not by what it thinks about the past or what it thinks could or should happen in the future. This demonstrates the importance of adapting to and accepting the circumstances of life as they arise.

Being fully aware of what is happening now without attaching to details allows us to flow with the natural unfolding of events, rather than resisting or trying to control them.

Some of us live our entire lives trying to straddle the gap between the past and the future and are terrified that if they let go of either, even for a moment, life as they know it will crash and burn. I like to use the analogy of selecting steppingstones to cross a brook

As children we would rush headlong and probably end up in the water. Some of us, having done that, are now terrified of crossing. But, with mindful awareness, we can test each stone to see if it will hold our weight before we move to the next stone. That way, we go safely all the way across.

IT IS IMPOSSIBLE TO FAIL IN MEDITATION

"Mindfulness means that we dwell completely on what we are doing without allowing ourselves to be distracted."

Dalai Lama

We sit with good intention. We try to relax and "be in the moment." We do our best to focus on our breath, or our seat, or our feet. Then we momentarily forget why we are sitting; why we are practicing. We go to sleep, or become bored, or feel irritated. Our egos squirm, distract, itch, and carry us off to far-away places or worry about the future. Then we have emotional reactions around what seems like our ego's non-compliance in spite of our good intentions. We feel like we are failing and just cannot meditate.

We become easily distracted because most of our life's experience is involved in *unconscious* reactions to people, places, or things. We have our normal way of looking at things, but that takes up very little bandwidth. The rest of our waking hours are involved in outside stimuli such as TV, radio, pets, children, shopping, cleaning, driving, thinking, worrying or the hundreds of other experiences we encounter on a daily basis.

In other words, it seems that we spend the majority of our time mindlessly waiting to react to something. To intervene with this habit, many of us are drawn to begin practicing meditation, which is the exact opposite of our usual *mindlessness* practice.

Meditation invites us to become still instead of active; to develop a single object focus instead of reacting to sights, sounds, smells, thoughts, or sensations; to begin slowing our thinking instead of trying to control what is as organized as a box of puppies.

One cannot fail in practicing meditation. Each session our experience becomes a little deeper, a little more calm, a little more relaxed. And a remarkable phenomenon related to meditation is that we always pick it back up where we left off the last time. Our bodies and minds are becoming accustomed to and comfortable with the practice.

We never have to "start over."

LETTING GO

"With every breath, the old moment is lost; a new moment arrives. We exhale and we let go of the old moment. It is lost to us. In doing so, we let go of the person we used to be. We inhale and breathe in the moment that is becoming. In doing so, we welcome the person we are becoming. We repeat the process. This is meditation. This is renewal. This is life."

Lama Surya Das

By Thich Nhat Hanh[29]

The first method of creating joy and happiness is to cast off, to leave behind. There is a kind of joy that comes from letting go. Many of us are bound to so many things. We believe these things are necessary for our survival, our security, and our happiness. But many of these things—or more precisely, our beliefs about their utter necessity—are really obstacles for our joy and happiness.

Sometimes you think that having a certain career, diploma, salary, house, or partner is crucial for your happiness. You think you can't go on without it. Even when you have achieved that situation, or are with that person, you continue to suffer. At the same time, you're still afraid that if you let go of that prize you've attained, it will be even worse; you will be even more miserable without the object you are clinging to. You can't live with it, and you can't live without it.

If you come to look deeply into your fearful attachment, you will realize that it is in fact the very obstacle to your joy and happiness. You have the capacity to let it go. Letting go takes a lot of courage sometimes. But once you let go, happiness comes very quickly. You won't have to go around searching for it.

Imagine you're a city dweller taking a weekend trip out to the countryside. If you live in a big metropolis, there's a lot of noise, dust,

---

[29] excerpted FROM: "5 Practices for Nurturing Happiness" by Thich Nat Hahn, 12 December 2022, IN LION'S ROAR magazine, March 2024

pollution, and odors, but also a lot of opportunities and excitement. One day, a friend coaxes you into getting away for a couple of days. At first you may say, "I can't. I have too much work. I might miss an important call."

But finally, he convinces you to leave, and an hour or two later, you find yourself in the countryside. You see open space. You see the sky, and you feel the breeze on your cheeks. Happiness is born from the fact that you could leave the city behind. If you hadn't left, how could you experience that kind of joy? You needed to let go.

EQUANIMITY – PART ONE

"Accepting the reality of change gives rise to equanimity."
Allan Lakos

"Equanimity can be defined as an even-minded mental state or dispositional tendency toward all experiences or objects, regardless of their origin or their affective valence (pleasant, unpleasant, or neutral)."[30]

We begin our meditations the same way each time… we set the intention, commit to the activity, arrange ourselves and environment for the practice, check our posture to establish a strong back and soft front and then engage.

From that point our meditation can vary depending on our training, experience, group, whether we are led or not or, walking or sitting. What follows is the result of our practice. We may be listening intently to a teacher or recording to tell us what to do or become aware of.

We may simply follow our breath as it comes in through the nostrils and flows out to dissipate. We may become acutely mindful of our feet and ankles as they touch the floor and release.

As we engage in our practice, we may notice phenomena (sounds, smells, emotions, thoughts) that come and go, and we may notice the gradually growing "gaps" between phenomena.

Wayne Dyer described this awareness as "falling into the space between." Our awareness seems to expand, and we simply become observers of our own minds and life as it exerts itself around us.

With practice, we learn to simply "be" and deepen that even-minded state of equanimity.

The more we continue a regular practice, we eventually realize that the practice slowly, but inevitably, merges with the life we experience when we are not formally meditating.

---

[30] FROM: https://www.ncbi.nlm.nih.gov/pmc/articles/PMC4350240/

We find that we become less upset or triggered by things that used to bother us; we become aware of things we have ignored, and we have less of a tendency to reach for or seek things that we think we don't have.

Equanimity has permeated our waking life.

Within that equanimity is a startling realization that, for the moment, we are not suffering, we feel peace, compassion stirs for others and we need nothing.

Life has become the meditation.

EQUANIMITY – PART TWO[31]

"Go placidly amid the noise and the haste and remember what peace there may be in silence."

Max Ehrman, Desiderata

What is equanimity, and how can we invite more of it into our lives? Equanimity is being willing and able to accept things as they are in this moment—whether they're challenging, boring, exciting, disappointing, painful, or exactly what we want. Equanimity brings calmness and balance to moments of joy as well as difficulty. It protects us from an emotional overreaction, allows us to rest in a bigger perspective, and contains a basic trust in the course of things.

Equanimity is like the eye of the storm, the calm center, that is grounded in the knowledge that everything is constantly changing and much of it is out of our control. The mature oak tree is another symbol of equanimity. Firmly rooted in the earth, it's not moved by the changing seasons and weather patterns. The tree owes this stability to its taproots, which anchor it securely so that it's stable but not rigid, even in strong storms.

We can ask ourselves: What are our taproots? What helps us withstand the inevitable storms of life? The Buddha warned against being taken in by the "eight worldly winds," which today, 2,600 years later, still blow back and forth: pleasure and pain, praise and blame, success and failure, profit, and loss. Of course we'd prefer to experience only one side of the winds, the side we see as positive, but the more we see that they shift again and again, the more deeply we can connect with our taproot.

Equanimity should not be confused with indifference. From the outside, these two conditions look confusingly similar, which is why

---

[31] Article excerpt FROM: How to Find Balance Through Equanimity by Christiane Wolf IN Lion's Roar 1 MAY 2024 (https://www.lionsroar.com/equanimity-finding-better-balance/)

in Buddhist literature indifference is referred to as the "close enemy" of equanimity. Equanimity isn't gritting your teeth or white knuckling it. Rather, it's caring deeply but with a sense of ease. Equanimity can only arise through the embodied acceptance of the fact that we don't have complete control over any given situation.

Equanimity and mindfulness are closely interwoven and mutually reinforcing, but they're two distinct skills that develop at different speeds. We can experience mindfulness from the beginning of our meditation practice, while equanimity often takes a little longer.

Being nonjudgmental is part of the definition of mindfulness. Yet when we begin to practice mindfulness, we become aware of how irritated, judgmental, unfriendly, and lacking in equanimity we often are. Ironically, it's the presence of mindfulness that makes us see this lack of equanimity clearly!

Through mindfulness we can observe the flow of thoughts, feelings, and sensations in the body without having a knee-jerk reaction. By repeatedly doing this practice, insights arise into the complex, often impersonal causal chains of experiences. These insights give us a greater perspective and lead to more equanimity. We can trust that if we regularly practice mindfulness and insight meditation, we'll naturally be more at ease.

"In meditation, focus on the present moment, and let go of all thoughts about the past or future."

Jon Kabat Zinn

I, like so many others, have watched the Olympics and admired the incredible feats of the athletes: Swimming, Gymnastics, Equestrian, Rowing, Track and Field and so many others. Humans like us that have discovered, or are discovering, the nearly unlimited capacity to physically, emotionally, and mentally excel, continue to pass even their own expectations. And, as I was caught up in these trials of excellence, it occurred to me that these incredible people have two things in common with us that meditate: Discipline and Focus.

It is possible that some of the athletes in the Olympics were genetically "selected" for their sport, meaning that for them, everything fell in place easily – health, support, finances, privilege. Based on the number of countries that sent participants to the games, I suspect that the "privileged" were few. For the majority, excellence comes from hard work, unwavering practice, and dedication. They prove, beyond any doubt, that with that level of determination, anyone can accomplish anything.

In sport, the participant learns to block out things that would impede the activity. Athletes learn to get into "the zone" where there is nothing else but their focus. Essentially, as their bodies are being conditioned, the athletes enter into a form of profound meditation in order to succeed.

As we know, meditation involves training the mind to concentrate and maintain focus on a chosen object, thought, or activity. Over time, participants and athletes alike find that discipline and dedication always pay off in expanded awareness, profound grounding, and increased capacity/ability. And, as the training deepens, it inadvertently helps and supports all others that they come in contact with. Once the individual learns to apply that focus, they can apply it to anything – education, science, spirituality, family and, of course, more sports.

There are only two things that separate the athlete and the meditator. That is, if for some reason the practice stops, is impeded or a rest period is necessary, the meditator picks back up exactly where they left off. The athlete has to go back and recondition the physical body. The second thing is what one wins in meditation practice is not a medal, but freedom from suffering. As an old guy now way beyond his athletic days, somehow this makes me feel better.

THE EAR DOOR[32]

"What benefit is there in forced meditation That is not free of the distraction of mind"

Tsangnyon Heruka[33]

By Jack Kornfield

"Meditation comes alive through a growing capacity to release our habitual entanglement in the stories and plans, conflicts and worries that make up the small sense of self, and to rest in awareness.

In meditation we do this simply by acknowledging the moment-to-moment changing conditions—the pleasure and pain, the praise and blame, the litany of ideas and expectations that arise.

Without identifying with them, we can rest in the awareness itself, beyond conditions, and experience what my teacher Ajahn Chah called *jai pongsai*, our natural lightness of heart. Developing this capacity to rest in awareness nourishes *samadhi* (concentration), which stabilizes and clarifies the mind, and *prajna* (wisdom), that sees things as they are… (…)

To amplify and deepen an understanding of how to practice with awareness as space, the following instructions can be helpful.

One of the most accessible ways to open to spacious awareness is through the ear door, listening to the sounds of the universe around us. Because the river of sound comes and goes so naturally, and is so obviously out of our control, listening brings the mind to a naturally balanced state of openness and attention.

I learned this particular practice of sound as a gateway to space from my colleague Joseph Goldstein more than 25 years ago and have used it ever since. Awareness of sound in space can be an excellent

---

[32] Excerpted from: Develop a Mind Like Sky by Jack Kornfield IN Lion's Roar Magazine, June 2024

[33] The Hundred Thousand Songs of Milarepa: A New Translation

way to begin practice because it initiates the sitting period with the flavor of wakeful ease and spacious letting go. Or it can be used after a period of focused attention.

Whenever you begin, sit comfortably and at ease. Let your body be at rest and your breathing be natural. Close your eyes. Take several full breaths and let each release gently. Allow yourself to be still.

Now shift awareness away from the breath. Begin to listen to the play of sounds around you. Notice those that are loud and soft, far, and near. Just listen. Notice how all sounds arise and vanish, leaving no trace. Listen for a time in a relaxed, open way.

As you listen, let yourself sense or imagine that your mind is not limited to your head. Sense that your mind is expanding to be like the sky—open, clear, vast like space.

There is no inside or outside. Let the awareness of your mind extend in every direction like the sky."

OTHER WAYS TO PRACTICE MEDITATION

"Everything in your life is a reflection of a choice you have made. If you want a different result, make a difference choice."

Anon

The following small article is written by Konda Mason in the July, 2023 issue of Lion's Roar Magazine which is a publication supporting Buddhist wisdom, thought, and instruction. Ms. Mason is a teacher at Spirit Rock Meditation Center and cofounder of Impact Hub Oakland, CA.

Question: I don't really like formal meditation that much, but I love going for contemplative walks, listening to beautiful music, reading Buddhist books, and other things that feel spiritual to me. Is it OK if I find other ways to be meditative besides sitting on a cushion following my breath?

Konda Mason: What a great question, and not an uncommon experience. Our world is filled with a plethora of wonder and beauty that ignites a sense of awe in so many ways. Walks in the woods, music, and the arts, sitting on the beach… this human experience is truly a gift filled with an abundance of opportunities to feel a sense of stillness and peace in our lives.

What happens with Vipassana meditation (that practiced at TMG) is oftentimes the opposite of peacefulness. The mind can become so busy in the so-called "stillness" that we feel we are doing it all wrong and would rather read about the dharma than actually meditate!

If you hang in there, though, this busy mind can become the doorway to experience insight, which is what the word Vipassana actually means. Over time, as you bring your awareness first to the breath, followed by the body, feelings, and thoughts, insight into the present moment, absent of preference or judgment, begins to emerge in mini increments.

These moments of insight are priceless! They can become an extremely useful tool in your everyday life as you navigate the internal and external challenges of being human.

So, I recommend do both: enjoy your meditative experiences off the cushion AND keep your curiosity ignited to explore the possibility of transformative insights that may occur from a regular meditation practice. Good luck!

"True education means providing an optimal environment in which each child's self-regulated learning process can unfold naturally. After all, the very word 'education' comes to us from the Latin educare, 'to lead out from within,' the highest qualities of each unique soul. In this process, meditation proves to be the most efficient and practical means."

Swami Satyananda

What will be the true legacy we leave our children? Will it be the same as what we received? Will they appreciate or dismiss it as we have? Will they take advantage or squander it as we did? With abundance or poverty, will they find peace? I am sure that for those of us in a parent's role, these considerations have or will arise at some point for all. For my children, I attempted to plant the seeds of mindful awareness as I was discovering it for myself. My hope is that the seeds grew in fertile ground and may be a legacy worth passing along.

Following are some excerpts from https://liveanddare.com/meditation-for-kids. Copyrighted content. "Bringing Meditation and Personal Growth to one million people" (Live and Dare mission).

"Childhood and teenage years are foundational in our development as human beings. It is when our personalities are formed, our view of the world developed, and our ways of relating to others and to ourselves established. The skills and tools we learn in our early years have a huge impact on the rest of our lives—and that is why meditation is such a great gift to give to a child....

The Benefits of Meditation for Kids:

- Better Behavior
- Less ADHD

- Better School Performance
- Less Stress and Depression

Meditation was also found to help kids improve their relationship with their parents, improve impulse control, build self-esteem, improve empathy and social skills, decrease test anxiety, and reduce post-traumatic symptoms…. With meditation, kids learn how to better manage their bodies, their energy, and their emotions. There is an increase in emotional intelligence, a positive outlook of life, and in the ability to regulate oneself. Kids develop better organizational skills and learn to be more present and less judgmental, responding rather than reacting to their life events. They feel better, learn better, and sleep better.

The skills that will come about as a result of meditation will unfold in many aspects of that child's life and will be carried over into the teenage years and on into adulthood. It becomes an integral part of their development and their resources for navigating the world. It helps set them up for a happier and healthier life.

How to Teach Meditation for Kids

Teaching kids is different from teaching adults. Kids have less patience, shorter attention span, and less capacity to sit still. On the other hand, they have a greater imagination, a sense of playfulness, and they learn by example.

As a result, in order to teach meditation effectively to kids, keep the following six principles in mind.

1. Make it Engaging and Fun
2. Appeal to Their Imagination
3. Keep it Short
4. Lead By Example
5. Be Flexible and Supportive
6. Manage Your Expectations"

IT'S SIMPLE

"In your investigation of the world, never allow the mind to desert the body. Examine its nature, see the elements that comprise it, kindly see the imperma- nence, the suffering, the selflessness of the body while sitting, standing, walking, or lying down. Then its true nature is seen fully and lucidly by the mind/heart; the wonders of the world become clear."

Ajahn Mun, Tibetan Meditation Master[34]

Meditation is probably one of the simplest acts of self-care one can do. Yet, for most people, even the *thought* of meditating stirs up the sympathetic, fight/fight/freeze mechanism when likely, they've never really given it an honest effort. Why is that? Speaking for my- self, although I had heard of meditation from the oogee-boogee crowd, I just could not bring myself to even attempt it until later in life. Winston Churchill was quoted as saying, "Americans will inevi- tably do the right thing… after they've done everything else." I am afraid that I was one of those Americans.

I decided to take meditation seriously when I came to the realiza- tion that I didn't find myself in trouble (suffering) every time I thought, but every time I found myself suffering, I had been thinking. In other words, I was my own worst enemy and I didn't know how to get around that. I had tried behavior modification, exercise, over- working, planned distraction, even going to counseling, but I could not shake the constantly compulsive, punishing ego that had some- how taken up residence in my head. Meditation was the only thing left to try.

The following is one of the practices I had run across that truly helped – it's really simple:

---

[34]   https://www.lionsroar.com/ask-the-teachers-what-does-it-mean-to-understand-bud- dhism-through-the-body/?goal=0_1988ee44b2-22a9649468-27752744

The Ticking Watch Meditation by Alex Kakuyo[35]

Required Items

1. An analog wristwatch with a second hand that ticks to count each second.

2. A comfortable place to sit.

Practice

1. Sit in a comfortable position.

2. Breathe in and out through your nose; extending the belly button on every inhale like you had a large meal and relaxing on every exhale

3. Look at your wristwatch and count each second until you get to 60.

4. If your mind wanders, say "hello" to your thoughts and bring your focus back to your watch.

5. At the end of 60 seconds, check-in" with your mind. If it feels agitated or unclear, go back to step two.

In this meditation there are two things that are happening. First, we engage our bodies to help calm our mind. Breathing in and out through the nose engages the parasympathetic nervous system, signaling to our minds that it's safe to relax. By pushing out our belly buttons on each inhale we expand our diaphragms, which helps us take in more oxygen. This also helps us relax.

Second, we take our watch as the object of concentration, using it to rob our negative thoughts of energy. Each time we count a passing second instead of dwelling on our thoughts we remove a log from the fire of our passions; letting them die away so peace can enter our minds.

---

[35] Alex Kakuyo is a Buddhist teacher and breathwork facilitator. A former Marine, he served in both Iraq and Afghanistan before finding the Dharma through a series of happy accidents. Alex holds a B.A. in philosophy from Wabash College and his life's work is helping students bridge the gap between the finite and the infinite. Using movement, meditation, and gratitude practices he helps them find inner peace in every moment. Alex is the author of *Perfectly Ordinary: Buddhist Teachings for Everyday Life*. IN https://www.lionsroar.com/ticking-watch-meditation/

Once our minds are at peace (or slightly less agitated at the very least), we're able to avoid self-created suffering by making better decisions and not giving energy to harmful emotions.

STACKING

"If we're really engaged in mindfulness when walking along the path to the village, then we will consider the act of each step we take as an infinite wonder, and a joy will open our hearts like a flower, enabling us to enter the world of reality"

Thich Nhat Hahn

Many of us have had the experience of a baby tightly gripping our fingers as we help them "stand." They seem to wobble about, but their bodies appear to "know" how to straighten the legs and seek some form of balance. If the baby is gently tilted in one direction or another, the baby will automatically shift their feet and legs to accommodate that direction. It's almost like "walking," but the baby is not thinking about it. It's just happy to smile and drool.

Here's a newsflash for many of us: Our bodies "know" how to do that too, though smiling and drooling has become optional for most. Many of us, however, seem to have taken our body's innate ability for granted and have lost both touch and confidence that they will do what they were programmed to do. In the growing complexity of life as an "adult," we seem to have isolated our minds away from that that supports them.

As an experiment, simply stand where you are. I invite you to notice the pressure points on the bottom of your feet. That invitation extends to noticing the tiny micromovements of the ankles and lower legs as balance is automatically maintained. After all, their job is to stabilize the lumpy hu-man stacked above.

Consciously tilt the pelvis so the low back is slightly flattened while slightly bending the knees. Notice how feet and legs relax into this position. Notice if there is a slight change to the pressure points on the soles of the feet. Straighten the shoulders into a strong-back-soft-front posture as the head is lifted slightly. Now notice the feet again.

Rest in that position for a moment. Simply rest and notice your breathing. Notice the stability of the structure that is "remembering" how to support that enormous head that thinks it knows everything. And breathe.

Now, shift the weight slowly and gently back and forth, front to back. Notice how the body is ready to automatically respond should a direction be chosen. This is called the "Sweet-Spot" or what I call *STACKING*. We place our feet on the floor and as we stand, *CONSCIOUSLY STACK* from the soles of our feet up to our head…and breathe.

Fundamentally, we use the same noticing and awareness in slow walking meditations. We notice how our bodies automatically change when we shift our weight; how the heel touches the ground and different pressure responses light up our feet; how our relaxed bodies sway automatically as we simply breathe and move.

From this position, we can start our day, or get out of our chair, or go to work, or greet others, or offer to help.

Gratitude can be found when we are stable and stacked. Confident in our momentary safety, we can become aware of what's around us and make solid choices moving forward.

We can relax and give the monkey mind a break from worrying and fretting and misinterpreting emotions. We can just be and maybe notice, in the process of "living," that daffodils are blooming…in spite of everything else.

How often do we pause for a moment to *REALLY* look at a daffodil?

BACK TO THE BEGINNING

"You can't stop the waves, but you can learn how to surf"

Jon Kabat Zinn

Mindfulness meditation has its roots in Buddhist teachings, but it is much more fundamental and secular. On that note, I found a simple, easy to practice instruction posted online at a website called VeryWellMind, a mental health education practice from New York (reference in the footnote).

I have included excerpts here:

How to Practice Mindfulness Meditation

Mindfulness meditation is a mental training practice that teaches you to slow down racing thoughts, let go of negativity, and calm both your mind and body. It combines meditation with the practice of mindfulness, which can be defined as a mental state that involves being fully focused on "the now" so you can acknowledge and accept your thoughts, feelings, and sensations without judgment.

Techniques can vary, but in general, mindfulness meditation involves deep breathing and awareness of body and mind. Practicing mindfulness meditation doesn't require props or preparation (no need for candles, essential oils, or mantras, unless you enjoy them). To get started, all you need is a comfortable place to sit, three to five minutes of free time, and a judgment-free mindset.

Get Comfortable

Find a quiet and comfortable place. Sit in a chair or on the floor with your head, neck, and back straight but not stiff. It's also helpful to wear comfortable, loose clothing so you're not distracted.

But being that this practice can be done anywhere for any amount of time, a dress code is not required.

Consider a Timer

While it's not necessary, a timer (preferably with a soft, gentle alarm) can help you focus on meditation and forget about time—and eliminate any excuses you have for stopping and doing something else.

While some people meditate for longer sessions, even a few minutes every day can make a difference. Begin with a short, 5-minute meditation session and increase your sessions by 10 or 15 minutes until you are comfortable meditating for 30 minutes at a time.

Focus on Breathing

Become aware of your breath, attuning to the sensation of air moving in and out of your body as you breathe. Feel your belly rise and fall as the air enters your nostrils and leaves your nostrils. Pay attention to the temperature change when the breath is inhaled versus when it's exhaled.

Notice Your Thoughts

The goal is not to stop your thoughts but to get more comfortable becoming the "witness" to the thoughts. When thoughts come up in your mind, don't ignore or suppress them. Simply note them, remain calm, and use your breathing as an anchor. Imagine your thoughts as clouds passing by; watch them float by as they shift and change. Repeat this as often as you need to while you are meditating.

Give Yourself a Break

If you find yourself getting carried away in your thoughts - whether with worry, fear, anxiety, or hope - observe where your mind went, without judgment, and just return to your breathing. Don't be hard on yourself if this happens; the practice of returning to your breath and refocusing on the present is the practice of mindfulness.

Download an App

If you're having trouble practicing mindfulness meditation on your own, consider downloading an app (like Calm or Headspace) that provides free meditations and teaches you a variety of tools to help you get centered throughout your day.[36]

---

[36] https://www.verywellmind.com/mindfulness-meditation-88369

THE CURE FOR THE PAIN IS THE PAIN

"To remain stable is to refrain from trying to separate yourself from a pain because you know that you cannot. Running away from fear is fear, fighting pain is pain, trying to be brave is being scared. If the mind is in pain, the mind is pain. The thinker has no other form than his thought. There is no escape."

Alan Wilson Watts[37]

By Esther Wakefield[38]

When the 13th-century poet, Rumi, tells us, *"The cure for pain is the pain,"* it can sound like one of those adult aphorisms I was annoyed with in childhood. You know, *"a penny saved is a penny earned,"* when I wanted to buy a candy bar with my pocket money. Or *"an ounce of prevention is worth a pound of cure,"* when I tried to get into the lake, but an adult was making me wait for my sunscreen to dry. Not my priorities! Why not spend the money, skip skin care, and just avoid the pain? And anyway, when I was told the cure for pain was the pain, it was usually by an adult walking ahead of me up the trail who didn't seem to understand that my pain was an emergency. It sounded like *"your pain isn't important to me, and stop telling me about it,"* and I was infuriated.

It wasn't until I had learned about distress tolerance training in graduate school that I could see the wisdom in this phrase. Distress tolerance is when you can sit with the discomfort, observe it, and not treat the sensation like an emergency to be acted upon immediately. The pain can be physical, emotional, or mental. Distress does some-

---

times need to be acted on! You might need to end the relationship, or make a doctor's appointment for a nagging twinge, or change your job. But sometimes distress is just how life goes, and nothing is wrong.

Being able to bear pain skillfully takes time and practice. Distress tolerance looks like responding after thinking instead of reacting immediately. It looks like persisting when things are uncomfortable. It looks like saying *"just because I feel bad doesn't mean anyone did anything wrong."*

My practice for tolerating pain uses mindfulness meditation. I sit and focus on my breath. I try to hold my attention on my breath lightly and still be aware of my body and surroundings. Trying to keep my attention on my breath, my mind wanders, and I notice I have shifted focus. *"Thinking,"* I notice my mind gently, and bring my mind back to my breath. This happens again and again.

I build up the skill of noticing when I am thinking. I build up the skill of observing myself in a way that is gentle and non-judgmental. I have had waves of emotional pain, annoyance, fear, and sadness wash through me while meditating. I get itchy, my body aches, and I might have a headache or allergies. I think *"I really should have been a plumber, I should tell Hannah about my idea for pesto, there's probably a pun about chicken stock and hosiery,"* and I can really get going! Still, I sit and keep bringing my mind back to my breath and the room.

I am more likely to notice my distress because I have practiced noticing my internal state. I can be uncomfortable, so I can hold off from immediately making myself comfortable. Making myself comfortable might look like hardening myself against others, being selfish, rude, or mean. I might insist on getting my way at work or be sitting on the couch and looking at my phone instead of helping out with the housework.

Making myself comfortable might also look like avoiding hard things, so I stay in a job I hate, or drink too much, or put up with mistreatment from a lousy friend or spouse. But, because I can notice my discomfort, I am less likely to react from a place of discomfort. I can pause and respond. I might need to compromise, or pitch in. I might need a divorce and a better job.

The cure for the noise, fear, and anger in my mind is sitting with the noise, fear, and anger of my mind.
The cure for pain is the pain.

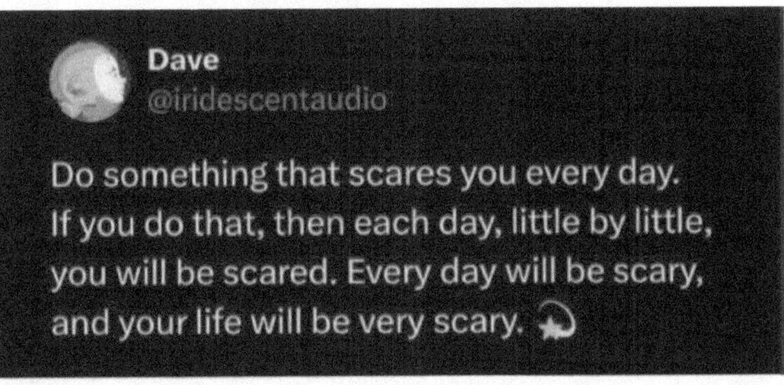

"Every morning, we are born again. What we do today is what matters most."

Buddha

Sol Naixent (pronounced *Sol Nashin*) in Catalan, a proto language for Spanish and French, simply means "rising sun." But in Barcelona within the autonomous community of Catalonia, "rising sun" has many connotations. It can mean "early morning." or it can mean "to awaken," or, my favorite, "a point of view" as described by Chögyam Trungpa Rinpoche. He contrasts the "rising sun mentality" with the "setting sun mentality" in his teachings. The rising sun mentality is associated with the Great Eastern Sun, representing a state of mind that is fully awake and radiant. This is in opposition to the setting sun mentality, which is characterized by a sense of loss, darkness, and despair.[39]

What better way to begin the day than by simply beginning. First thing in the morning, simply smile. Have a glass of cool water. Smile again for no particular reason. Maybe you don't feel like smiling. Do it anyway for just a moment. Interestingly, it takes far fewer fascial muscles to smile than to frown. It actually takes a lot of effort to frown and keep our faces stuck that way. So, in a way, smiling can actually give our faces a break from all that effort.

Developing Kindness toward Yourself — A Metta Practice

• Close your eyes, ground yourself on your seat. Make sure you are fully supported, and your feet are placed firmly on the ground.
• Become aware of the breath permeating your body. Imagine it to be a spray clearing the toxins from your heart.

---

[39]https://search.brave.com/search?q=trungpa+rinpoche+quote+about+rising+sun+mentality&source=desktop&summary=1&conversation=2e62efacc20a7afe0b7a2f

• After a minute try to visualize looking back at yourself or see yourself in a beautiful place that you enjoy. Or just silently call your name. Remember to breathe.

• After another minute say to yourself, "May I be happy," then breathe and acknowledge how this feels. Then say, "May I be well," then breathe and acknowledge how this feels. Then say, "May I be kind toward my suffering," then breathe.

• Allow yourself to sit in stillness with whatever arises. After a few minutes say, "May I cultivate more kindness within my heart. May I cultivate more peace within my heart. May I continue to develop and grow."

• Continue to recite these phrases, leaving a minute or two between each, staying connected with yourself all the time.

• After ten minutes, bring the practice to an end.[40]

If you practice this weekly it will begin to transform your heart. If you do it daily it will bring about positive change in your life. If our hearts are full of love and kindness for ourselves, there is little room for anger. Such mental states might arise, but love is the cleansing water that puts out the flames of anger.

And another day begins *con Sol Naixent.*

---

[40] IN https://www.lionsroar.com/a-practice-for-developing-kindness-toward-yourself/ BY **Valerie Mason-John**, a senior teacher in the Triratna Order and author of *Detox Your Heart: Meditations for Emotional Trauma.*

ASTEROIDS

"It is better to conquer yourself than to win a thousand battles. Then the victory is yours. It cannot be taken from you."

Buddha

Back when I was young and full(er) of myself, before the public internet, cell phones, or thoughts of sobriety, fledgling computer game companies like Atari began putting game consoles out in public. The purpose was to harvest people's extra change, but they were momentarily entertaining and were particularly prevalent on US military bases where I and others like me stumbled upon them.

There was Pong, Galaga, Pinball, Asteroids, etc., and with paychecks in our pockets begging to be spent, we gladly obliged by releasing most of them through these games… and a lot of beer. Honestly, we were clueless. We were not aware that even back then, we were being gently offered a real-time metaphor on how to work with overwhelming thoughts, emotions, and life itself.

Asteroids, in particular placed "you" in a 2-dimensional spaceship in "space" which was a blank screen. "You" could change direction a little and "move" slowly using a trackball on the console.

Your objective was to not get smashed by "asteroids" - other 2-dimensional things randomly moving about in space. You could shoot the asteroids to break them up and protect yourself, but any size asteroid could smash you, so blowing up big ones increased your chances of being overwhelmed and smashed by little ones. You gained "points" by essentially surviving.

In meditation, at least initially, we follow our breath and relax into our posture. For most of us, it doesn't take long for our monkey-minds to come up with a thought (asteroid).

Maybe we can just let it go by and go back to our breathing. But, if we engage with that thought (shoot it), it inevitably breaks into other related thoughts and, before we know it, we are overwhelmed with a kaleidoscopic panorama and momentarily forget why we are sitting there in the first place. Then we have to start over (put in another quarter.) We have been hooked by a pattern as old as man.

The difference between Asteroids and meditation though, is that meditation doesn't require quarters and thoughts are not "real." In neuroscience, they are closer to virtual ball-lightning storms happening all over our brains that we have attached meaning to.

In other words, if we do not engage with them, our "ship" is not going to blow up and we're not going to die. We will eventually be left "alone" in "space" of our own making.

One of the chief reasons that people do not catch on to the beauty of meditation is that they are afraid to be "alone." Which is also why a lot of folks are attracted to video games. None of them have experienced the safety and unconditional love found in their own "space."

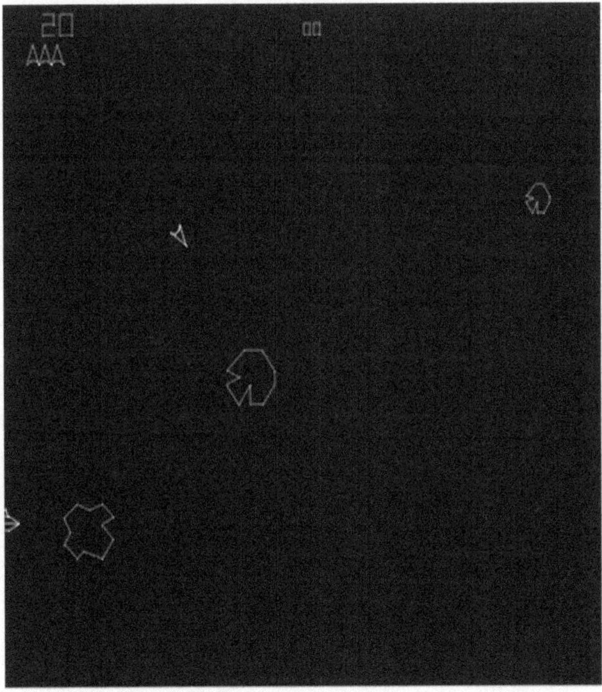

"We are birthed into sangha, into sacred community. It is called the world."

Adyashanti

by Thich Nhat Hahn

"A sangha is a community of friends practicing (…) together in order to bring about and to maintain awareness. The essence of a sangha is awareness, understanding, acceptance, harmony, and love. When you do not see these in a community, it is not a true sangha, and you should have the courage to say so. But when you find these elements are present in a community, you know that you have the happiness and fortune of being in a real sangha.

(…) Our modern society creates so many young people without roots. They are uprooted from their families and their society; they wander around, not quite human beings, because they do not have roots. Quite a number of them come from broken families and feel rejected by society. They live on the margins, looking for a home, for something to belong to. They are like trees without roots.

For these people, it's very difficult to practice. A tree without roots cannot absorb anything; it cannot survive. Even if they practice intensively for ten years, it's very hard for them to be transformed if they remain an island if they cannot establish a link with other people.

A community of practice, a sangha, can provide a second chance to a young person who comes from a broken family or is alienated from his or her society. If the community of practice is organized as a family with a friendly, warm atmosphere, young people can succeed in their practice.

(…) Our civilization, our culture, has been characterized by individualism. The individual wants to be free from the society, from

---

the family. The individual does not think he or she needs to take refuge in the family or in the society and thinks that he or she can be happy without a sangha. That is why we do not have solidity, we do not have harmony, we do not have the communication that we so need.

The practice is, therefore, to grow some roots. The sangha is not a place to hide in order to avoid your responsibilities. The sangha is a place to practice for the transformation and the healing of self and society. When you are strong, you can be there in order to help society. If your society is in trouble, if your family is broken, if your church is no longer capable of providing you with spiritual life, then you work to take refuge in the sangha so that you can restore your strength, your understanding, your compassion, your confidence.

And then in turn you can use that strength, understanding and compassion to rebuild your family and society, to renew your church, to restore communication and harmony.

This can only be done as a community—not as an individual, but as a sangha.

"Meditation brings wisdom, lack of mediation leaves ignorance. Know well what leads you forward and what holds you back and choose the path that leads to wisdom."

Buddha

"The main objective of meditating in a group is to create an energy field where the whole is greater than the sum of the parts," says Susan Shumsky, meditation instructor, and author of *Exploring Meditation*.

"In other words, when one person meditates alone, there is a feeling of expanded awareness, deep relaxation, peace of mind, and contentment. When many people meditate together, those experiences are intensified, and effects expand to the environment. So, benefits are both individual and collective."

Along with expanding your mind and sense of awareness while practicing group meditation, some believe there is a biological and chemical occurrence that happens when people choose to meditate together.

According to Ellie Shoja, founder of Peace Unleashed, "We are all vibrational beings having physical experiences. And as such, we are all connected. The easiest way to see the effect of this interconnectedness is when you witness someone you care about experiencing something. If they're experiencing joy, you're more likely to experience joy with them. If they're in pain, it might physically hurt you to be in the vicinity of their pain.

"When we meditate, our vibration naturally rises. When we meditate in a group setting, we have an opportunity to experience the clarity of someone else's raised vibrations. This is why, for first-time meditators, being in a group can be comforting. Because even if they are not able to quiet their own thoughts enough to allow their own vibration to rise, they can take advantage of being in the vibrational vicinity of the raised vibrations of more seasoned meditators around them."

Meditation in itself is a personal journey that reflects on clearing your mind and focusing on each breath. But when practicing meditation within a group setting, you're able to feed off the energy of the group.

According to (others),
"Meditation is always an individual journey because it's a journey into the self. However, the group allows us to go deeper into ourselves. We're able to take advantage of the group's high vibrations to raise our own beyond our immediate ability. It's important to have an individual, daily practice. Periodic group sits, however, can complement the private practice and help us dig deeper into ourselves than we can individually."[42]

---

[42] FROM: https://aaptiv.com/magazine/group-meditation-sessions

HEALING

"Simply bringing awareness to the process of breathing initiates the release of peptide molecules from the hindbrain to regulate breathing while unifying all systems."

Candice Pert, Ph D.

With your attention lightly on the sensation around your nose, breathe in slowly and breathe out. Breathe in and breathe out. Allow the air to permeate your systems. Watch the old, stale air dissipate into the world. All senses alive but attached to nothing like watching passing clouds from an airplane as you notice your body breathing in and out.

Imagine that you are breathing through the pores of your skin, slowly in and out. With the in-breath, the body slightly expands and with the out-breath, the body watches the spent air dissipate. All senses are alive as your body breathes.

Dr. Candace Pert (1946-2013), a neuroscientist from Georgetown University, said that the smallest level of consciousness is the single cell of the body. Neurochemically, the cell is conscious of what it needs and disposes of what it doesn't need. There are mechanisms within it that maintain a fine balance so the cell can remain healthy and vital as it works in conjunction with adjacent cells for a purpose greater than itself.

Dr. Pert goes on to say,

" My research has shown me that when emotions are expressed-which is to say that the biochemicals that are the substrate of emotion are flowing freely - all systems are united and made whole. When emotions are repressed, denied, and not allowed to be whatever they may be, our network pathways get blocked, stopping the flow of the vital feel-good, unifying chemicals that run both our biology and our behavior."[43]

---

[43] *Molecules of Emotion: Why You Feel the Way You Feel*, Scribner, 1997

In other words, it has been shown that emotionally, your mind is in every cell of your body; the body and mind are not separate. The chemicals that run the body and mind are the same as those that are involved in emotions – emotions are the glue that holds the cells together. Your body *is* your subconscious mind.

When we meditate and disengage from impermanent phenomena (things that come and go), we are integrating our systems into conscious unity. From that balance, it is not difficult to observe our thoughts and emotions and to see patterns that serve us or don't. They are simply part of the flow within that unity – as is the air and external sensations in our environment.

From that temporary disconnected view, we are free to have compassion for the incredible resilience our bodies have demonstrated when beset by our out-of-whack thoughts and emotions. Now we can gently work with them like we would an untrained puppy.

Now, as we breathe, we can love and heal.

BEING STILL

"The outer world comprises situations, people and their behavior, relation-ships, work, material possessions, natural resources and even our body (or physical health). The inner world comprises thoughts, feelings, intentions, and memories."

BK Shivani

Newborn babies are mostly observers, lacking references, or a sense of self until about age two. At that point, all education and experience is focused on the outer world. Because of that outer world view, many of us have developed a sense of self that is defined by our external interactive experience and is often a comparison to either other people or our past.

Culturally, there seems to be little guidance on managing one's inner world and individually, our experience there is based on personal interpretation, habit, or reaction. It's no wonder why researchers suggest that stress, more than almost anything else, contributes to declining physical and mental health.

BK Shivani, a teacher from the Indian Brahma Kumari tradition offers some remarkably clear and simple teachings on how to approach this outer world/inner world dilemma. As quoted above, she outlines what comprises the outer world and points out that we fundamentally have no control over whatever happens outside of ourselves.

Certainly, we have choices and intentions, but much like shooting an arrow from a bow, the endpoint of our choices and intentions may be not what we expected.

Shivani goes on to suggest that the only things we DO have control over is the inner world, where our thoughts, feelings, intentions, and memories lie. Through awareness and discipline, we can divert habitual thought patterns into more positive and altruistic channels thereby creating a better lived experience. And, of course, the very best way to practice this diversion is through meditation.

In meditation, we are not trying to get rid of anything or create something we don't have. We are simply being still, quiet, and aware. Thoughts, emotions, and memories come and go within the space of our awareness.

In the practice outlined above, we can become alert to certain "flavors" of thought and emotion and provide an antidote to those that feel low or are not conducive to our wellbeing. As we practice in meditation, it becomes easier to pause and reflect on what we may be projecting into the world around us, particularly when we are not in meditation.

The key to all of this though, is learning to be comfortable in stillness. This may seem difficult to a mind that is totally programmed into "doing."

In our beautiful little community of Tamworth, NH, we have become acquainted with Janet Legro who also puts out a simple, philosophical newsletter called *"Centering Prayer – Tuesday Letter"* that wonderfully parallels Breathing Room in many ways. It seems that in one issue, in particular, we seem to be on the same page when it comes to stillness. She referenced Thomas Merton and his belief that "time in silence helps one gain not only perspective but also humility."[44]

As we sit, or walk, silence flows through us, surrounds us, supports us, sustains us, and protects us. All of our thoughts, feelings, intentions, and memories arise from that silence where we have an opportunity to simply observe them before they re-emerge with the silence.

In that space, we can learn to refine whatever is forthcoming, discern truth, and discard whatever is not relevant to our well-being. But becoming comfortable in the stillness is key.

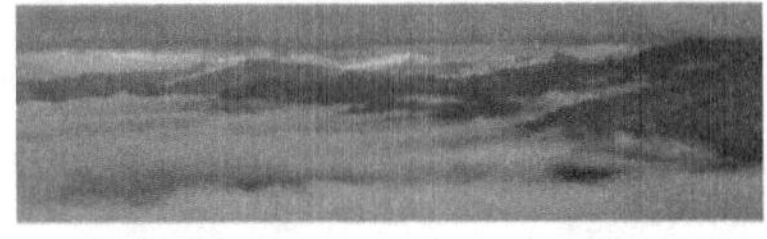

---

[44] Janet Legro, "Centering Prayer-Tuesday Letter", Aug 26, 2025

THE GAP

"If you change the way you look at things, the things you look at change"

Wayne Dyer

We all are familiar with the children's song "Itsy – Bitsy Spider" that was sung to us when we were little. It is a simple song with an easy-to-follow tune. Each note has a specific tone and measure/gap (how long it lasts) in order to follow along with and enjoy the song.

Similarly, the words of this sentence are made up of letters (tones) put together to give meaning with a gap in between each word to provide timing. What if there were no gaps?

Whatwouldthesentencelooklikeiftherewerenogaps?

The sentence might be difficult without the gaps between words, and we might be easily overwhelmed as we try to understand. The same goes for music, conversation, events, our own thoughts and even meditation. Without some form of gap, everything would be presented as overwhelming chaos.

Yet, as we focus on *things* (notes, clouds, words, history, thoughts, etc.) we are usually not aware of the gaps between.

As an experiment, unfocus your eyes just a little as you read this page and notice how the gaps jump out at you. As a matter of fact, there are way *more* gaps than words here. There is an entire blank page that the words float on.

Unfocus a little more and the words resemble birds flying in a vast sky. We are programmed to see only the words. Thoughts and images in our minds are like that too. We were never taught to rest between our thoughts.

Meditation is a practice of falling into "the gaps." It takes a little practice, but once you get the hang of it, you realize you have a place to really rest. It helps with sleeping issues also!

Wayne Dyer said,

> *"The paramount reason for daily meditation is to get into the gap between our thoughts and make conscious contact with the creative energy of life itself."*

THE BEAUTY OF SILENCE IN MEDITATION

"You can hear the footsteps of God when silence reigns in the mind."

Sri Satya Sai Baba

One of the places I grew up was in the silence of the high desert and between the Rockies and the Sierra Nevada mountains. They surrounded the Great Basin which, millions of years ago, was once the inland sea, Lahontan. It is a vast living desert a mile above sea level and its physical presence is enough to boost anyone's imagination.

As a small child, I physically felt the silence of the vast landscape and soaring peaks. It seemed to push in on my eardrums and helped me feel calm and focused and inclusive to those that knew its secret… that it wasn't so much silent as selective. The little sounds that one heard were private messages and only for the one who heard them. The wind rustling the sagebrush; the skittering of a blue-belly lizard; the little pebble falling into the arroyo; all quiet messages from the Universe inviting me to breathe in the rosemary after the rain and be at peace because I truly belonged… to all of it.

Now I realize that the silence was a sanctuary where I could be safe; where I felt secure, where a fist would not follow someone else's rage. As I grew up, the times of silence grew further apart until at some point I became permanently distracted from the messages and became used to dancing with constant noise. It was not until decades later that silence was reintroduced to my life and I remembered.

Much, much later in life, I was introduced to Shamata Vipassana, a simple form of meditation whose name means *Peaceful Abiding*. I was gently shown how to let the noise and distractions of the world and the discursiveness of the mind just flow on by because it is all impermanent phenomena; it appears and disappears with gaps between. What I was sitting on was solid, what I was standing on was solid, but those things too, in time, would become impermanent. With practice

I became aware that the silence I had remembered and experienced as a child manifested in those gaps like sunlight between Venetian blinds.

When we first begin to practice meditation, silence can seem illusive because of what we are normally accustomed to. Yet I invite all to consider that everything else may just be a sonic illusion that keeps us from knowing who we are; that keeps us distracted and afraid.

When we realize that the silence is our foundation; that it has no beginning or end, we can float within it like a chip of wood floating on the water. We are safe, we are warm, and we are held in the arms of the Universe.

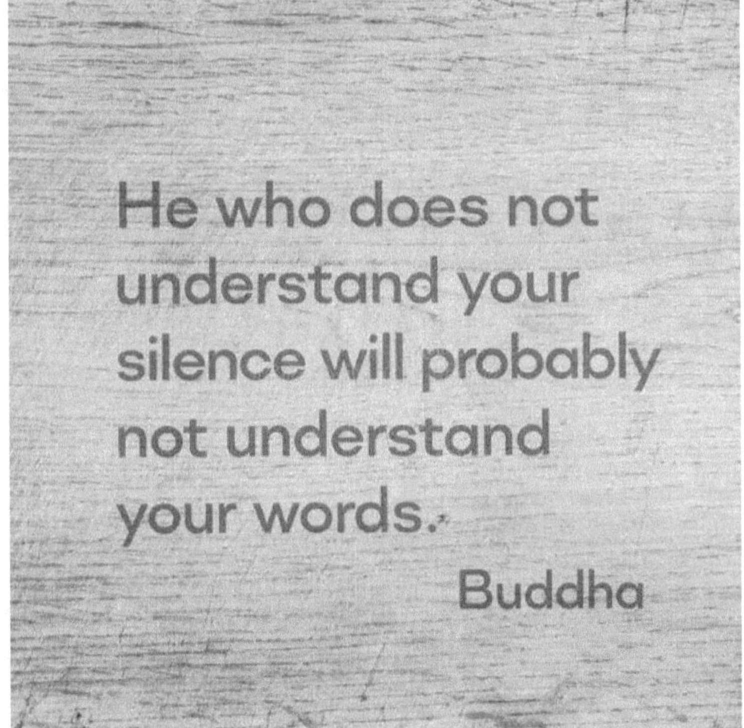

LOVING KINDNESS

"Loving-kindness (Maitri in Sanskrit, Metta in Pali) is not simply a quality we have. It is an important Buddhist meditation that we can learn to practice regularly, and the most powerful form of generating healthiness. Loving-kindness, along with compassion, sympathetic joy, and equanimity, is one of the four immeasurable attitudes that heal the temporary ills of our life and awaken the enlightened qualities that we all have inherited."

Tulku Thondup Rinpoche

By Pema Chodron[45]

"In meditation we discover our inherent restlessness. Sometimes we get up and leave. Sometimes we sit there but our bodies wiggle and squirm and our minds go far away. This can be so uncomfortable that we feel it's impossible to stay.

Yet this feeling can teach us not just about ourselves, but what it is to be human…we really don't want to stay with the nakedness of our present experience. It goes against the grain to stay present.

These are the times when only gentleness and a sense of humor can give us the strength to settle down…so whenever we wander off, we gently encourage ourselves to "stay" and settle down.

Are we experiencing restlessness? Stay! Are fear and loathing out of control? Stay! Aching knees and throbbing back? Stay! What's for lunch? Stay! I can't stand this another minute! Stay!"

---

[45] Pema Chödrön, The Places That Scare You: A Guide to Fearlessness in Difficult Times, Shambhala 2002

OUR INTENT AND OUR EXPERIENCE

"Personally, I've found that words and text limit how I experience what goes beyond words and text. If you want someone to experience the moon, the best descriptions are not as good as simply walking outside and pointing silently at the moon."

Rev. Eli Brown-Stevenson[46]

Putting together and writing these pieces is a privilege that I do not take lightly. On one hand, I very much enjoy the process of allowing subject material to arise naturally. On the other hand, I keep in mind my original intent of helping to provide encouragement and content to those that are exploring mindfulness meditation for the first time. But I also know, and name, that *this* brain/ego can easily get carried away and end up complicating the simplicity of meditative practice.

The beauty of this practice, and all of life, for that matter, is found in the *contemplation* of the lived experience. As the Reverend Eli Brown-Stevenson said above

"…words and text limit how I experience what goes beyond words and text."

Today, I invite you to set an intent. Once every waking hour stop what you are doing for one minute and simply notice your breath as it comes in and goes out. Try not to put all your attention on the breath, just notice what it is doing for that minute as you simply become aware of whatever else is going on.

Feel the air around you; notice sounds and smells; become aware of whatever is touching your body. Become quiet for just one minute

---

each hour. After that minute, I invite you to contemplate your experience of that single minute as you go about the rest of that hour. I think you'll be pleasantly surprised at what you discover.

In the process of putting words and text to this page, I find the usual whirlwind of my "monkey-mind" trying to be precise, trying to be detailed, trying to fill every nook and cranny with the "right" things to say.

But as I pause for my "minute" simply noticing my breath, I feel a small smile arising. The air is fresh, my body is comfortable, I feel, for this minute, happy to be here.

"You could just be here. Instead of being not here, instead of being absorbed in thinking, planning, and worrying, instead of being caught up in the cocoon, cut off from your sense perceptions, cut off from the power and magic of the moment, you could be here."

Pema Chodron

It's funny to me how the beauty of this experience works. At 5:00 AM, I woke up with a full agenda in my head, busy sorting what to do when and knowing full well that the deadline for this manuscript was eminent. Bathroom, coffee, computer, sit, sip, think, then a random sound stopped me for a moment. Then I noticed the mist rising from the humidifier and the curtain moving gently from the little fan.

Just for a moment, I was pulled from my cocoon before I plunged back into my go-to online resource for a lot of my material around meditation, *Lion's Roar Magazine*. Right there, the first thing my eyes were drawn to is the January 13th, 2025, article[47] written by Pema Chodron around EXACTLY what my mind was doing from the time I woke up… and the familiar remedy that I had momentarily forgotten.

Unfortunately, there is no space here to present the entire article, so I have excerpted some of it hoping to encourage you to cut and paste the link and read it in its entirety yourself. This is important. Maybe, today, the most important thing you do. Maybe not.

"… () When we realize that we are hooked, that we're on automatic pilot, what do we do next? That is a central question for the practitioner… () One of the most effective means for working with that moment when we see the gathering storm of our habitual tenden-

---

[47] https://www.lionsroar.com/waking-up-to-your-world-pema-chodron/

cies is the practice of pausing or creating a gap. We can stop and take three conscious breaths, and the world has a chance to open up to us in that gap. We can allow space into our state of mind.

Before I talk more about consciously pausing or creating a gap, it might be helpful to appreciate the gap that already exists in our environment. Awakened mind exists in our surroundings — in the air and the wind, in the sea, in the land, in the animals — but how often are we actually touching in with it? Are we poking our heads out of our cocoons long enough to actually taste it, experience it, let it shift something in us, let it penetrate our conventional way of looking at things?

If you take some time to formally practice meditation, perhaps in the early morning, there is a lot of silence and space. Meditation practice itself is a way to create gaps. Every time you realize you are thinking, and you let your thoughts go, you are creating a gap. Every time the breath goes out, you are creating a gap. You may not always experience it that way, but the basic meditation instruction is designed to be full of gaps. If you don't fill up your practice time with your discursive mind, with your worrying and obsessing and all that kind of thing, you have time to experience the blessing of your surroundings. You can just sit there quietly. Then maybe silence will dawn on you, and the sacredness of the space will penetrate.

Or maybe not. Maybe you are already caught up in the work you have to do that day, the projects you haven't finished from the day before. Maybe you worry about something that has to be done, or hasn't been done, or a letter that you just received. Maybe you are caught up in busy mind, caught up in hesitation or fear, depression, or discouragement. In other words, you've gone into your cocoon.

For all of us, the experience of our entanglement differs from day to day. Nevertheless, if you connect with the blessings of your surroundings — the stillness, the magic, and the power — maybe that feeling can stay with you and you can go into your day with it. Whatever it is you are doing, the magic, the sacredness, the expansiveness, the stillness, stays with you. When you are in touch with that larger environment, it can cut through your cocoon mentality."

I hope that you cut and paste the link provided in the reference at the bottom of the previous page. It only takes a couple of minutes to read. You may find the experience worthwhile.

R.A.I.N. MEDITATION

" We take a step back from being in the midst of the experience to become aware that the experience is happening. This creates a small but meaningful distance between ourselves and the emotion, which is the first step toward greater emotional freedom.

Gullu Singh

Developed by Michele McDonald and popularized by Tara Brach, RAIN is an acronym representing four steps in meditation practice: recognize, allow, investigate, and nonidentification (or nurture). The RAIN meditation method can be applied to any experience, but it's particularly useful for working with difficult emotions like anxiety.[48]

1. Recognize

The first step in the RAIN process is to recognize what's happening. Recognizing the present moment might seem simple, but anxiety has a way of hijacking our attention and flooding us with a deluge of thoughts and fears. (…) The recognition that comes with mindfulness allows us step out of our entanglement with anxiety. We take a step back from being in the midst of the experience to become aware that the experience is happening. (…) Recognition is not about trying to change or fix anything; it's simply about becoming aware. Without clear awareness, we're vulnerable to habituated, unhelpful coping strategies such as distraction, busyness, or unhealthy self-soothing… (…) which may provide temporary relief but do not address the root cause of our distress… (…) if we want to change our experience, identifying the difficult emotion is crucial.

2. Allow the Experience

---

[48] Excerpted from **How to Practice RAIN Meditation for Anxiety** by Gulu Singh IN https://www.lionsroar.com/how-to-practice-rain-meditation-for-anxiety

Allowing means softening and opening to the experience of anxiety, just as it is. (...) This acceptance doesn't mean we approve of or enjoy the feeling; it's just acknowledging that it is true in this moment. (...) This isn't about resignation, but rather a wise recognition that resisting difficult emotions only amplifies their intensity. (...) By allowing the emotion to be there for the moment and not struggling with it, it becomes easier to manage.

3. Investigate

The triangle of awareness is a useful framework for investigation. The triangle of awareness refers to the three components of any experience: thoughts, emotions, and physical sensations. By examining the experience of anxiety from these three perspectives, we deconstruct anxiety in a way that makes the discomfort more tolerable and the overall experience more manageable. (...) ... we notice the story that plays in the mind when anxiety is present. (...)

Next, notice if there are other recognizable emotions in the midst of anxiety. Fear, anger, guilt, shame, frustration, loneliness, which often coexist with and exacerbate the feeling of anxiety. Again, allow these emotions to be here and allow yourself to feel them, as best as you are able. (...)

Finally, focus on feeling the physical sensations associated with anxiety. (...) Notice where each experience resides in the body. Does it have a shape? What's the texture or flavor of this experience? Is it solid and static, or is it changing? Where in the body does it feel difficult or unpleasant or painful? (...)

When we practice resting in the felt sense of anxiety, allowing it to be just as it is, a remarkable transformation occurs over time. The familiar discomfort of anxiety loses some of its sting. We realize that anxiety, like any other sensation, is impermanent. It rises and falls, and we can tolerate it. In this acceptance, there's a profound sense of freedom.

4. Nonidentification or Nurture

The final step in the RAIN process is nonidentification—not identifying with anxiety. This doesn't mean denying it or pretending it doesn't exist; it means realizing that anxiety is not who we are, but rather just something we experience. This shift in perspective often reveals itself in our language. Instead of saying, "I'm anxious," we might observe, "I'm aware of anxiety." This subtle change signifies a profound transformation in our consciousness. (…)

After we have recognized, allowed, and investigated our experience, we can offer ourselves some kindness and compassion. (…) Nurturing helps to soften the experience and bring a sense of warmth and care to our practice. It's a reminder that mindfulness isn't just about observing our experience, but also about relating to it with compassion.

The beauty of RAIN lies in its accessibility—it's a tool you can use anytime, anyplace, and in any challenging situation. The more you practice, the more it becomes an instinctive response that transforms your relationship with anxiety and other difficult emotions. (…) The gift of RAIN is not the elimination of life's challenges, but the cultivation of ways to meet them with greater ease and grace.

"If mindfulness is the practice of tending to our experience directly, then when we pay attention, it turns out we become more, not less, sensitive to the events of life."

Ethan Nichtern[49]

Back in 2014, I volunteered for the Veterans Hospital at the Hooksett Vet Center near Manchester, NH. I was introducing mindfulness meditation to combat veterans as a way to help them through PTSD and other issues. At the time, I began putting a little booklet together called "Take Your Seat" which I hoped would prove helpful as a little booklet if it ever emerged from my computer. Well, I got distracted, and it is still there. Recently, I found that somebody kind of beat me to the title, at least in an article form. Our good friend Meredeth Young Sowers said, *"If you have a good idea, get it out there where others can see it. If you don't, somebody else will."* Swallowing my hubris, I offer excerpts of "How Mindfulness Builds Confidence" by Ethan Nichtern here. The full link in Lions Roar is below.

"… In Buddhism… () … forces that both inflate and deflate our self-regard are sometimes called the eight worldly winds, because they can blow us off balance. They can also be thought of as eight traps of hope and fear, because we're trapped in constantly chasing after them or bracing against them. The historical Buddha categorized the eight worldly winds into four couplets, in which the first of each pair represents our elation (what we reach for) and the second describes our deflation (what we try to avoid). These are the four pairs of worldly winds:

---

[49] https://www.lionsroar.com/how-mindfulness-builds-confidence/

1. pleasure/pain
2. praise/criticism
3. fame/insignificance
4. success/failure (or gain/loss)

… In Buddhism, the skill to recognize and face these forces goes by the name *upekkha*. This term is often confusingly translated as "equanimity." Equanimity is almost always a head-scratcher for students. In English, it has the connotation of non-disturbance, inertia, or stillness. But if you meditate for more than five seconds, you come to the realization that there is no stillness, either internally or externally. Relative stillness certainly exists: Life in the country may be calmer than life in the city, but absolute stillness does not exist in our world. Even skyscrapers are built to sway in the wind. If you're paying attention when any of the eight winds start to blow, you're going to feel them, and they're going to push you in a certain direction.

… "Take your seat" is used as a shorthand instruction for arranging one's meditative posture. On the surface level, it describes the physical entry into contemplative practice. We find a long spine and an open heart, assume a confident but receptive demeanor, and balance alertness with physical relaxation. The posture was intuitively designed to balance the parasympathetic and sympathetic nervous systems and quell our "fight, flight, or freeze" response long enough to help us grow more curious and insightful about our internal experience. The posture—upright but not uptight, as my colleague and friend Maho Kawachi likes to say—is designed to help us find the physical alignment that lets us experience our mental events in a state of (relatively) nonjudgmental awareness…

… "Take your seat" also has a deeper meaning that extends far beyond meditation practice. It's an empowering instruction for how to show up on this earth. "Take your seat" grants us permission to take up space with confidence—not arrogance. It's about having a sense of our own worth and owning our capabilities without self-diminishment… () "Taking your seat," or true presence, happens when you accept the disappointment of not being able to escape your humanity. The thudding return to earth—coming back to yourself exactly as you are—happens not just once, but repeatedly. This disappointment is exactly what Buddhist meditation compels us to embrace and, eventually, transform into happiness, to use an extremely controversial word. Once you accept your non-transcendence, the feeling of being stuck with your flawed humanity turns into a deep sense of relief. You can give up trying to either disappear or become someone else. You become more able to inhabit both the joys and the frustrations of being a citizen of this planet at this time of chaos. The failure to transcend everyday experience is not the malfunctioning of practice; it's the start of the journey."

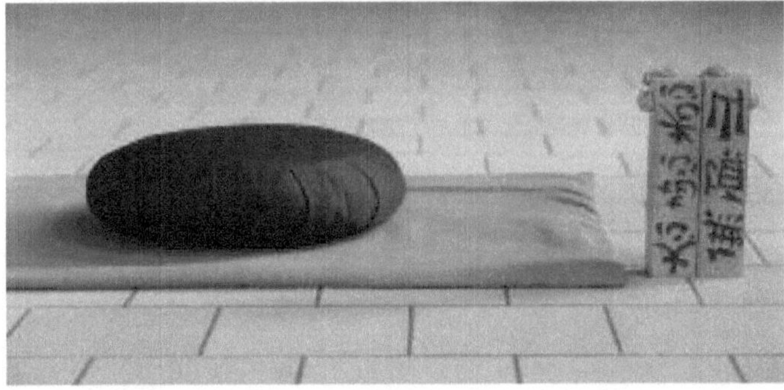

."Breath by breath, let go of fear, expectation, anger, regret, cravings, frustration, fatigue. Let go of the need for approval. Let go of old judgments and opinions. Die to all that and fly free. Soar in the freedom of desire-lessness. Let's go. Let Be. See through everything and be free, complete, luminous, at home -- at ease.""

Lama Surya Das

We have been talking widely around the practice of meditation and some of the teachings and philosophy behind the practice, but sometimes, with good intent, accidentally open the door allowing bored monkey-minds to go off into the weeds a little bit. With a smile, a breath, and a fresh start, we come back to the practice. Here are excerpts from a Sharon Salzberg piece in *Lion's Roar*[50] that is exactly about that.

"Sit comfortably on a cushion or a chair. Keep your back erect, but without straining or overarching. (If you can't sit, lie on your back, on a yoga mat or folded blanket, with your arms at your sides.)

Close your eyes if you're comfortable with that. If not, gaze gently a few feet in front of you. Aim for a state of alert relaxation.

Deliberately take three or four deep breaths, feeling the air as it enters your nostrils, fills your chest and abdomen, and flows out again. Then let your breathing settle into its natural rhythm, without forcing or controlling it. Just feel the breath as it happens, without

---

trying to change it or improve it. You're breathing anyway. All you have to do is feel it.

… () … Let your attention rest on the feeling of the natural breath, one breath at a time. (Notice how often the word "rest" comes up in this instruction? This is a very restful practice.) You don't need to change it, force it, or "do it right": just feel it. You don't need to make the breath deeper or longer or different from the way it is. Simply be aware of it, one breath at a time.

You may find that the rhythm of your breathing changes. Just allow it to be however it is. Sometimes people get a little self-conscious, almost panicky, about watching themselves breathe—they start hyperventilating a little or holding their breath without fully realizing what they're doing. If that happens, just breathe more gently. To help support your awareness of the breath, you might want to experiment with silently saying to yourself "in" with each inhalation and "out" with each exhalation, or perhaps "rising" and "falling." But make this mental note very quietly within, so that you don't disrupt your concentration on the sensations of the breath.

Many distractions will arise—thoughts, images, emotions, aches, pains, plans. Just be with your breath and let them go. You don't need to chase after them, you don't need to hang onto them, you don't need to analyze them. You're just breathing. Connecting to your breath when thoughts or images arise is like spotting a friend in a crowd: You don't have to shove everyone else aside or order them to go away; you just direct your attention, your enthusiasm, your interest toward your friend. "Oh," you think, "there's my friend in that crowd. Oh, there's my breath, among those thoughts and feelings and sensations." If distractions arise that are strong enough to take your attention away from the feeling of the breath—physical sensations, emotions, memories, plans, an incredible fantasy, a pressing list of chores, whatever it might be—or if you find that you've dozed off, don't be concerned. See if you can let go of any distractions and return your attention to the feeling of the breath.

… ◯ … The moment you realize you've been distracted is the magic moment. It's a chance to be really different, to try a new response. Rather than tell yourself you're weak or undisciplined, or give up in frustration, simply let go and begin again. In fact, instead of chastising yourself, you might thank yourself for recognizing that you've been distracted, and for returning to your breath. This act of beginning again is the essential art of the meditation practice.

Every time you find yourself speculating about the future, replaying the past, or getting wrapped up in self-criticism, shepherd your attention back to the actual sensations of the breath. If it helps restore concentration, mentally say "in" and "out" with each breath, as suggested earlier. Our practice is to let go gently and return to focusing on the breath. Note the word "gently." We gently acknowledge and release distractions and gently forgive ourselves for having wandered. With great kindness to ourselves, we once more return our attention to the breath.

You don't have to get mad at yourself for having a thought. You don't have to evaluate its content, just acknowledge it. You're not elaborating on the thought or feeling. You're not judging it. You're neither struggling against it nor falling into its embrace and getting swept away by it. When you notice your mind is not on your breath, notice what is on your mind. And then, no matter what it is, let go of it. Come back to focusing on your nostrils or your abdomen or wherever you feel your breath.

If you have to let go of distractions and begin again thousands of times, fine. That's not a roadblock to the practice—that is the practice. That's life: starting over, one breath at a time."

CAN YOU HEAR IT?

"The bell of mindfulness is the voice of the Buddha calling us back to ourselves. We have to respect each sound of the bell, stop our thinking and talking, and get in touch with ourselves, breathing and smiling. This is not a Buddha from the outside. It is our own Buddha calling us home."

Thich Nhat Hanh

As I begin to write this piece, I take a breath, release it, and look around the small bedroom partially set up to be an office. If one were to apply a description of the room as a whole, words like clutter, disorganization and limited space might come to mind. But, in its way its contents are eclectic. In one way it is the flotsam of lives in transition, swept up in the rush to relocate to another "steppingstone" to whatever is next in life.

In another way, each part and piece stacked around was once central and precious, something to hold for the imagined important role it will play in the future. Around the desk and the space carved out to hold it are books, computers and their retinue of wires, monitors, printers and the like, and the nest I have created to sit and meditate.

The teachings say that one's meditation space does not HAVE to look like anything in particular. It just has to remain somewhat consistent so that, as one develops the habit of sitting, the body/mind knows what to expect. I have a few special pictures of loved ones and a few small representative statues, or murtis. I have a little statue of St. Francis to remind me that humility is the vehicle for service. Another is of Archangel Michael to encourage fortitude when the "demons" rummaging around in my head get out of hand. Ganesh reminds me that no problem is unsolvable and the little statues of Buddha here and there, each reflecting a different face of contemplation. But the ones my eyes track to most often are images of The Way

Shower reminding me to be kind and compassionate with myself as I come to terms with the impermanence of my own experience.

When I sit in my space, my posture aligned and my breath slowing, I can just be. There's no one else there but me and when I close my eyes, the reminders will be waiting should my eyes fall in that direction when they open. I can just be. The bell begins my time out of time and sounds again when it's time to take the yoke back up for another day. I trust the bell. If it's morning, I begin the day from there. If it's at night, the bell reminds me to go brush my teeth before bed. Following something said by Thich Nhat Han, it is easy to imagine the sound of the bell permeating the universe as a herald to compassion and peace. And throughout the day, if I take a moment to become still, I can call up its sound; I can hear its call reverberating; I can stop, listen, and be at peace.

RELATIONSHIPS

*"…if you find yourself having to choose between a relationship and a
practice that supports you, I would find myself questioning the nature of the
relationship."*

Susan Piver

Even now, a quarter of the way through the 21st century, a
random conversation about the benefits of a personal meditation
practice is often met with passing interest. At least it is not an alien
concept, but like Yoga or Tai Chi, finding the time to imvest means
cutting out really important things, like worry or overwhelm. Inviting
a practice into our lives is opening ourselves to a new relationship,
and because we are familiar with how relationships have gone in the
past, this can be scary. Even scarier, is that this relationship is with
ourselves, warts and all.

Even after decades of seeking and developing a diligent
practice, opening a relationship with myself has proven the most
daunting. I have had no problem taking personal inventory and
looking at behavioral patterns through introspection. I have even
gone to extreme lengths to "whip myself" into shape as necessary. I
found I could "play my part," but there has always been a deep place
within me that I just could not open up to share with another person,
or even with myself, for that matter. I haven't been able to trust what
what I could not see or touch. I do remember hearing something
about *emotional intelligence*, but I also remember just blowing it off at
the time.

The only thing I've found that even approaches touching
that "forbidden place" has been metta practice. Here is a wonderful
tool from Lisa Ernst, meditation teacher, artist and founder of One
Dharma Nashville. I exerpted parts of this from the February, 2025
issue of Lion's Roar Magazine.

How to Practice Loving-Kindness for Yourself

Settle into your posture. Notice how your body feels on the floor, chair, or cushion. Let your attention settle into the body.

Focus on your breathing. Notice the sensations of inhaling and exhaling wherever you feel them most strongly. For a few moments just rest with the breath, perhaps feeling a sense of ease, equanimity, and restfulness.

Now locate any emotions you feel in this moment as sensations in the body. Perhaps there's tightness in the throat, a heaviness in the heart, tension in the shoulders, or perhaps you feel at ease. Whatever you find, just **allow your feelings to be as they are**. If you find it difficult to stay present, widen your attention to include the entire body. If you'd like, place your hand at your heart and feel the care and kindness you can offer yourself in this moment.

Now, silently **repeat metta phrases**. Here are a few suggested phrases. You can choose all or any that speak to you:

> *May I be safe.*
> *May I be peaceful.*
> *May I be kind to myself.*
> *May I accept myself as I am in this moment.*
> *May I be held in compassion.*
> *May I be filled with loving-kindness.*
> *May I find joy and equanimity in this moment, just as it is.*

Get in touch with the intention of the words—to offer kindness, compassion, and acceptance. But don't force it. As your mind wanders, gently refresh the phrases in your heart. Do your best to offer yourself the same kindness, support, and acceptance you'd give a friend who's struggling. Can you meet all parts of yourself with kindness, nothing left out? If you're not yet ready, just hold this as an intention and do your best within your capacity, without judgment.

To close the practice, if you like, **extend the compassion outward** to all beings by repeating these phrases:

May we all be free of pain and sorrow.
May we all be held in compassion.
May we all be safe and at peace.

RETURN TO SHENPA

"The most difficult times for many of us are the ones we give ourselves"

Pema Chodron

At a quarter to five this morning, I was up and making my coffee. I do that. I naturally get up early. Life seems quieter then and my monkey-mind has yet to reach "full-tilt-boogie" status. It does that, you know. Just by itself. Most of the time, I take advantage of the quiet to just sit and observe my breath. It's easier when everything still seems asleep. Oh, there are house noises and tinnitus, but they are always there. And sometimes I just let my monkey-mind go wandering about like a dog exploring new smells in the yard. That's easy too.

So, this morning I was feeling a restless undercurrent and, just to put the inevitable off a little longer, I stepped outside into the chill darkness and smelled the forest smells and listened to the forest beginning to awaken, and I looked up at the stars. For a few minutes, my monkey mind was watching with me before it decided there was nothing stinky out there and it begged to wander somewhere else. With it pulling at the leash, I came back inside. I don't think the forest noticed. It had reached that gap between the "in-breath" of night and the "out-breath" of morning. That beautiful space that always was, always is and always will be.

In Tibetan, the word *shenpa*, loosely meaning "hook," is described as something that unconsciously causes us to react, to tighten, and to shut down, keeping us in cycles of dissatisfaction and suffering. Sound familiar? Pema Chodron says, "*shenpa* thrives on the underlying insecurity of living in a world that is always changing. We experience this insecurity as a background of slight unease or restlessness (tightening)."

It is constantly manifesting as an "urge." It might be an urge to move, stretch, escape, react. Or actually, it could be anything that disturbs.

The antidote for shenpa begins with the willingness to fully acknowledge our urge (an itch?), and then the willingness not to act on it (scratch it). Simply refrain from following through in that moment. Pema goes on to say,

"Without meditation practice, this is almost impossible to do. Generally speaking, we don't catch the tightening until we've indulged the urge to scratch our itch in some habitual way (…) In practicing with *shenpa*, first we try to recognize it. The best place to do this is on the meditation cushion.

Sitting practice teaches us how to open and relax to whatever arises, without picking and choosing. It teaches us to experience the uneasiness and the urge fully, and to interrupt the momentum that usually follows. We do this by not following after the thoughts and learning to come back to the present moment. We learn to stay with the uneasiness, the tightening, the itch of *shenpa*.

We train in sitting still with our desire to scratch. This is how we learn to stop the chain reaction of habitual patterns that otherwise will rule our lives. This is how we weaken the patterns that keep us hooked into discomfort that we mistake as comfort. We label the spinoff "thinking" and return to the present moment. Yet even in meditation, we experience *shenpa*."[51]

---

[51] https://www.lionsroar.com/how-we-get-hooked-shenpa-and-how-we-get-unhooked/

The experience I started this piece with is an example of what NOT to do when training with shenpa. If I was going to walk this morning's talk, I would have sat with the restlessness rather than engaging with it. I would have simply noticed it, then would have gone back to my breath. But it was early.

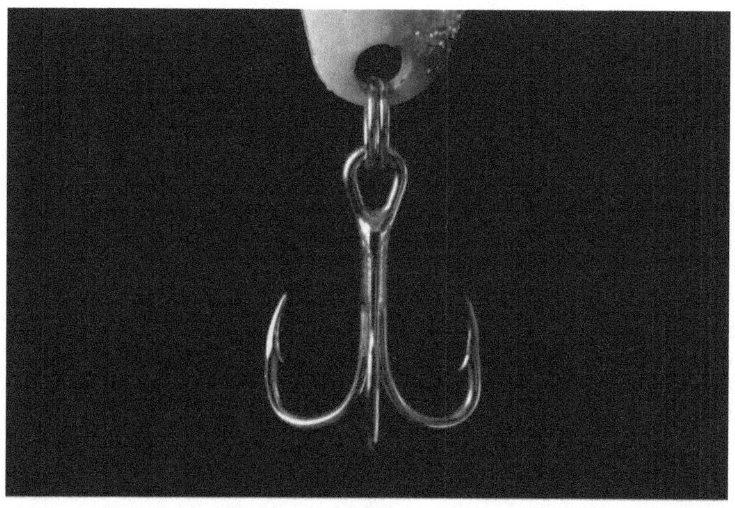

AGGREGATION (Klesha)

"Give a man a fish, and you feed him for a day. Teach a man to fish, and you feed him for a lifetime"

Anon

Shenpa, or "the hook," was introduced in the previous pages to hopefully bring awareness to urges that take us away from our "spot" at the moment that they happen. They can be anything that diverts our attention from whatever we are focused on until the moment we become aware we've been diverted. Something worth mentioning is that the moment we realize our attention has wandered, a tiny "gap" appears before we bring our attention back. At first, we don't notice it, but over time, as our awareness increases, noticing the "gap" can shift the way we perceive our ongoing experience. This is often termed *realization*.

This subject is something directly related to *shenpa* and, if not addressed, can stand in the way of not only meditation practice, but is considered one of the root causes of chronic suffering. *Shenpa* is superficial while **Klesha**, a Tibetan word representing an "aggregation" or "knot," is made up of layers of reactive emotions that may have been accumulating for years. With awareness, we can see that most of our superficial distractions carry an accompanying emotion. Maybe they present as an irritation, or a trigger of some sort. Or maybe, after we pick the shenpa "scab" off, we find worry, concern, or resentment hiding under the surface just waiting for an opening. The main purpose of meditation, as well as all the practices related to it, is to notice shenpa and uproot the kleshas so we are not bothered by them. But, if nothing happens to the kleshas over time, the practice isn't working.

Kleshas exploit unexamined insecurities by giving us a pre-packaged set of unconscious responses—ignoring, embracing, rejecting, and countless variations on those themes—that make sure we will never experience a fresh moment of openness. Some folks may tend to just clench their teeth as they ride through them, and some folks just bury them as a universal feeling of stress. With practice, we can become aware of them as we return to our "spot." But these things have been accumulating and have often become the foundation for our unconscious and habitual reactions to everything. Buddhists call this *Samsara*, the eternal cycle of birth, suffering, death, and rebirth[52] which is also a description of our cause-and-effect experiences throughout life.

"Learning on the cushion how to relate with these states inwardly does tend to give us a little more space when they arise in daily life. That little bit of space gives us more choices about whether to remain quiet, whether to speak, and if we speak, what to say. We start to develop the fine art of letting go inwardly while being restrained outwardly… By working with the kleshas, we learn lots of beautiful qualities, like humility and patience. The forbearance we practice just to be with a klesha without doing anything with it, strengthens our compassion. We see how the kleshas make us suffer, and therefore we understand the impact they have on others, which strengthens our determination to purify our hearts further. As we have success in doing that, it gives rise to faith and confidence as well.[53]"

Above, I have referenced an illuminating article from Lion's Roar Magazine that goes into much more depth than I have here. I invite you to take a look - It is a fascinating read.

---

[52] FROM The American Heritage® Dictionary of the English Language, 5th Edition

[53] https://www.lionsroar.com/forum-are-kleshas-obstacles-or-opportunities-for-enlightenment/

BOREDOM

"I never really understood what he said but every now and then I find myself barking with the dog, or bending with the irises, or helping out in other little ways"

Leonard Cohen

The above poem was written by Leonard Cohen, a poet, author, musician and Zen practitioner. The poem was a compliment to his teacher, Kyozan Joshu Sasaki who was the Roshi at the Mount Baldy Zen Center where Cohen spent a period of reclusion. I thought this quote was apt because it beautifully reveals an antidote to a challenge that all meditators run into - boredom.

Continuing and maintaining a meditation practice requires discipline and training. It is true that the training can be found in many places from in-person to personal experimentation, but the best training comes from a living teacher who can guide and advise the students as they begin to establish the discipline necessary to maintain a solid practice. Boredom in its many forms, can knock students "off their cushion" quickly and, if indulged, can make practice difficult if there is not someone to talk to about it. Without a teacher, students must navigate through challenges using the same mind that seems to punish them for trying to ignore it.

Teachings that I recall outline two types of boredom, both of which are emotions. ***"Hot"*** boredom presents as restlessness, itchiness, and a stream of rapid thought patterns looking for something "to do." For most of us, our entire waking focus is constantly on doing, accomplishing, sorting, judging, remembering, avoiding or projecting. To simply sit without "doing" seems almost unconscionable and alien. Without an agenda, our minds stimulate a form of anxiety; a felt sense of something wrong, that says we have somehow become vulnerable.

The second type is "**Cool**" boredom, or lethargy. We experience this emotion when our minds tell us if there's *nothing we can do*, we might as well give up, and surrender to circumstance. The most common manifestation of cool boredom is "sleepitation" – we just nod off into dreamland, sometimes almost falling off of our chair or cushion. Our minds can just wander into the distance just like at night when we lay down to rest.

Meditation has often been described as resting in an awakened state where we are deeply focusing on an object, a breath, or, in my experience, the space (sky) that holds all else within itself. I was taught that a thought or emotion is something that briefly catches our attention, but usually no more so than anything else that shows up in that space. If something seems to be persistent, simply observing it lightly and welcoming it as it is, often reveals layers that support it which can also be welcomed. In hot boredom, if there seems to be too much going on, closing the eyes can reduce outside stimulation and provide more space. In cool boredom, opening the eyes a little allows more environmental input and can be useful when we notice advancing lethargy. The eyes can be like the apertures in a camera lens accommodating light to clarify a picture.

Without taking liberties, I feel that the poem above illustrates our expanding awareness as we welcome and gently move *through* boredom. Peacefully abiding, we notice the barking of the dog. As we mindfully awaken, we can feel the bending of the irises. And as witness to life within and around us, we become that life, helping out in little ways.

BEING VERSUS DOING

"Meditation is simply sitting still without thinking"

Zen Saying

Within the context of meditation, the distinction between *being* and *doing* is both subtle and profound. *Doing* is the familiar mode in which most of us spend our days—planning, striving, achieving, checking off boxes on an endless to-do list. It is the active engagement with the world, the effort to shape experience, to push for change, to reach goals.

Being, on the other hand, asks us to step outside this constant motion. It is the gentle art of presence, an invitation to release the compulsion to act, fix, or improve. In being, we surrender the need to accomplish and simply allow ourselves to exist as we are, moment by moment. There is nothing to add, nothing to subtract; instead, there is space to observe, breathe, and accept.

Meditation is where these two modes meet—and where being is given its due. When we practice sitting quietly, we are cultivating the rare and nourishing state of simply being. This is not passivity, but a deep engagement with ourselves and our surroundings, without the filter of action or ambition. In being, clarity emerges, and with it, compassion and connection.

Building a meditation habit need not be complicated or daunting; in fact, the simplest practices are often the most effective. Setting aside a few moments each day to sit quietly, observe your breath, or listen to the sounds around you creates a gentle rhythm that naturally nurtures mindfulness. Even the act of returning to your cushion or chair—no matter how distracted or restless you feel—becomes a small victory, affirming your commitment and inviting a sense of ease.

Over time, these understated rituals become deeply rewarding. The repetition itself cultivates comfort, and each session brings its own subtle gifts: a single breath of peace, a fleeting moment of clarity, or the pleasure of simply pausing amid life's busy flow. In the company of others or in solitude, the habit grows, offering roots and renewal to your practice, one simple sitting at a time.

Find a time of the day you can stick to for a few minutes. Set a timer that helps you honor the time you have committed to the practice – 3 minutes, 5 minutes, 20 minutes, whatever you are comfortable with. Sit on a cushion or chair comfortably with your back straight and balanced – not too tight, not too loose. Imagine that you are being gently pulled upright by the crown of your head.

With your mouth slightly open, your gaze about six feet in front, notice your breath as it flows into and out of your body. Your hands are on your thighs or the left softly cupping the right in your lap with your thumbs touching. Listen intently to the sounds around you and notice that the sounds, the thoughts, your breathing are all taking place within the space around you.

Rest in that space just noticing until the timer calls you back. Ending your meditation when it still feels good is, itself, an intrinsic reward that encourages you to repeat the process.

Pause for a moment.

Notice the breath moving in and out.

Nothing needs to change.

Just this.

Even in uncertain weather,
the ground remains beneath us
and the sky remains above.

DISCIPLINE

"To enjoy good health, to bring true happiness to one's family, to bring peace to all, one must first discipline and control one's own mind. If a man can control his mind he can find the way to Enlightenment, and all wisdom and virtue will naturally come to him."

Buddha

Many people seem to understand *discipline* as something necessarily applied to young ones that lack it. In other words, it could be construed as a punishment or consequence to behavior. I suppose, from a child's point of view, that would be true because "just being a child" doesn't always fit into every social context. Now if that child were to grow up with that understanding, then discipline would probably be best avoided if possible.

On the other hand, if that child really wanted to excel in something, then the child would learn to practice specific skills in order to become proficient. That form of discipline carries reward rather than punishment. Its unfolding success could be of great benefit should the child choose to continue.

As adults, most of us have had some experience with both definitions. Self-esteem, worldview, or experience would color whichever definition would be dominant. My personal experience of a childhood in the 60's before going into the military seemed to lean toward the discipline-as-punishment overview.

Later, as I became interested in developing proficiency in some areas of life, I found it was not easy. I had to overcome layers of punishment-narrative, time constraints and day-sapping responsibilities if I wanted to progress. At some point, it almost became disheartening because other than the rigid discipline I had acquired in the military, discipline was lacking in my life and mind. I didn't realize that I had become reactive to "life" rather than flowing with it.

Life itself presents its own requirements. In order to be a good parent, I had to learn forms of self-discipline in order to refine what my parents had passed to me. In order to be financially responsible, new skills had to be acquired and practiced. And to remain healthy, I needed to develop discernment and diligence in my search for adequate nutrition. Frankly, developing those skills was a hit-or-miss endeavor, but I'm still here, debts are paid, and the kids grew up without too much resentment…I think.

At times throughout life, though, I think most of us "hear" something undefinable; something that seems to try to get our attention; something that seems to offer an alternative view to what our habits present. At some point, most of us think we have to go somewhere or see somebody or do something extraordinary to be able to hear it a little better, only to become disappointed because we can't seem to "catch" it. Some give up the search… some just keep searching and reaching and grasping.

What would it be like to consider that "it" has always been with us from the beginning? What if what was being whispered was simply "be still"? If that's the case, it's no wonder we couldn't hear it.

Being still is the opposite to what our culture and monkey minds demand and what does that even mean, anyway? Be still. Sounds pretty boring and besides, how can anything get done if we're being still? And yet there it is…whisper quiet…everywhere… if we listen.

As a matter of fact, it seems that everyone and everything we are aware of emerges from that stillness. What if this were Life itself gently offering an invitation?

All it would take is desire and a little discipline. Are you ready to listen?

"In Japan we have the phrase, "Shoshin," which means "beginner's mind." Our "original mind" includes everything within itself. It is always rich and sufficient within itself. This does not mean a closed mind, but actually an empty mind and a ready mind. If your mind is empty, it is always ready for anything. It is open to everything. In the beginner's mind there are many possibilities; in the expert's mind there are few."

Shunryu Suzuki[54]

The above quote is from a famous Zen Roshi (Master), Shunryu Suzuki. Suzuki states,

"In the zazen (meditation) posture, your mind and body have great power to accept things as they are, whether agreeable or disagreeable."

A beginner's mind is likened to the mind of a baby that carries no preconceived notions, ideas, or expectations. A baby is simply aware of "what is" and responds accordingly. If the child is not hungry, uncomfortable, tired, or sick, the child looks at the world with fresh eyes, interested in everything, but attached to none of it.

In the beginner's mind there is no thought "I have attained something." All self-centered thoughts limit our vast mind. When we have no thought of achievement, no thought of self, we are true beginners. Then we can really learn something"[55]

As we continue to practice, it becomes easier to just be aware of the present moment the more we practice it. Suzuki also said,

---

[54] FROM: Zen Mind, Beginner's Mind: Informal Talks on Zen Meditation and Practice
[55] FROM: https://www.dailyzen.com/journal/zen-mind-beginners-mind/

In her book, Interior Castles, about the life of St. Theresa of Avila, Mirabai Starr quotes the 15th century Carmelite nun describing practice as an intent which underlines Suzuki's acceptance statement above:

"This magnificent refuge is inside you. Enter… Close your eyes and follow your breath to the still place that leads you home."[56]

Beginning a meditation practice can seem fraught with peril. We are constantly being distracted by "poisonous vipers." Do I have to join a religion? What am I actually *doing*? How can I just sit here doing nothing for 20 minutes? I get anxiety when I'm not thinking about stuff! How do I empty my mind? What is my goal or purpose just sitting here like this? What do they mean by accepting things as they are? At least in Walking meditation, I'm doing stuff! Are we there yet?

Certainly, as adults, we have plans, tasks, and responsibilities in our daily lives. But most of these are done on "automatic pilot" where, as we are doing them, we are already thinking about something else. This can lead to quite a noisy experience. An added Beginner's Mind practice invites us to see all the things we missed when our minds were caught up in never-ending "stuff." There is a sense of freedom we didn't know we had as our focus gently retreats to the here and now and is no longer caught up in our past and future worries and concerns.

---

56 https://www.goodreads.com/book/show/868846.St_Teresa_of_Avila

SOLITUDE

"Solitude is very different from a 'time-out' from our busy lives. Solitude is the very ground from which community grows. Whenever we pray alone, study, read, write, or simply spend quiet time away from the places where we interact with each other directly, we are potentially opened for a deeper intimacy with each other."

Henri Nouwen

It is a shame that, to many people, the concept of meditation seems like one of those "entertainment" practices one does when one has nothing else to do. But who can blame them? Busyness seems to be required in our culture if we want to avoid external and internal judgement. With this kind of pressure, the compulsion to either be active or asleep is strong. To many, the best practice is to keep moving, keep doing, keep producing lest we be judged as lazy, selfish, indolent, or incompetent. We can sleep when we're done... except we're never done

.

Solitude and silence, if we're not accustomed to it, can be downright scary. That is one of the reasons folks have the tv or music going as white noise in the background. For city dwellers, it's almost a necessity so that they don't have to hear the neighbors or traffic or sirens. Folks moving from there to the country, forests or mountains tend to feel quite uncomfortable until they become used to the reduced noise and activity. And, in the high deserts of the West, where it feels like the natural solitude and silence presses upon the eardrums, the experience can be unnerving.

So, what would it be like to be truly quiet; to feel safe and comfortable and be simply aware without distraction? What would it be like to simply be in that space for a little while having dropped obsessions and compulsions and anxiety and narratives around what and why? With a little practice, it is easy to do and can provide a momentary intervention where we can rest while remaining fully awake. Solitude is not *out there*. Thomas Merton said,

"Solitude is not something you must hope for in the future. Rather, it is a deepening of the present, and unless you look for it in the present you will never find it."

Pema Chodron suggests starting from where we are, as we are, without judgement. To some it may seem impossible, to others, a waste of time.

Our sanity depends on the natural ebb and flow of stimulus, of information. We become accustomed (habituated) to speed of input, but if we receive too much too quickly, we become overwhelmed and anxious. If the stimulus is too slow, we either fall asleep or become bored and anxious. In some primitive way, it's likely a survival skill, but in this day and age, is it necessary? Meditation, whether sitting, laying down or walking, can help release us from the hamster wheel of constant input and offer peace and solitude in one place.

"It can be counterintuitive to relax when there is chaos. Yet learning to recognize, accept, investigate, and not identify with our experience—think of the mnemonic device "RAIN"—helps free us from the false realities our thoughts, emotions, and body sensations create. We usually feel that our experience is solid and will never change, but with insight it all breaks down into a million different aspects. We open so that all experience is a flowing stream, and when debris floats by, it is held with loving, non-judgmental, mindful awareness."[57]

In solitude, it's just us, warts, and all. In solitude, peace opens within us as we begin to notice that the silence is not something we

---

[57] BY Emily Horn, 7 June 2024 IN https://www.lionsroar.com/insight-meditation-present-open-aware/

must create or achieve. It is already here—surrounding us, flowing through us, protecting, and sustaining us—quietly holding everything that arises. We are not separate from it. Like the sky that contains clouds, birds, weather, and light without effort, this silence holds us in the same way. With a subtle shift in perspective, nothing needs to change and nothing needs to be added. In that moment, we are no different than the tree, the cloud, or the bird—each resting in what already is. And for as long as this is noticed, there is a simple sense of freedom.

Over time I noticed the practice becoming quieter.

Not because the world grows silent, but because I've mostly
stopped struggling with every sound and thought.

Outside, here in the forest, I don't feel small. I feel protected,
held, and embraced. I can smell the cleanliness of the air as I walk
among friends. The five tall oaks seem like sentinels welcoming me
into the real world where things are… just as they are.

My thoughts, as usual, want to flit here and there like little winter
birds. Hidden, then so fast, then hidden. Sometimes, I miss them
completely.

And sometimes I notice just in time. It makes me want to laugh if I
catch it fast enough. There is time for that… later… Because all I
have at these times, when I'm paying attention, are these moments
strung together into the tapestry of now.

And there is a quiet upwelling of gratitude — simply for having
stayed with this life long enough to notice. Life continues to happen
whether I participate or not.

Breath comes and goes. Thoughts come and go.

Even in uncertain weather, the ground remains beneath us and
the sky remains above

As my path continues, I offer a gentle invitation to consider pausing when you can as I am continually learning to do. Simply pause and breathe. Remarkably, nothing actually changes. Life continues as it does, but, for a moment, we get to simply watch.

There is an innate business to life all around as things grow and change and rise and fall. If we can take a moment to watch it seems that there is nothing that is not somehow active in some form or fashion. But between things, there is space and quiet. I sometimes wonder at why it takes so long before we can see that. It has been there all along.

Your experience is uniquely your own. Your own flavors, your own colors, your own interpretations that blend together into your lived experience. But if you are reading this, you are not done yet. There's more out there waiting for you to notice. There is a huge space within which all that is happening. Can you sense it?

Sometimes I wonder what it might be like to actually anticipate what we don't know? What might it be like to expand our awareness beyond what we are used to and embrace something beyond? It might actually be interesting.

But many of us discover that nothing extraordinary happens. Life continues — dishes, conversations, weather, ordinary days. But now we begin noticing these little gaps between the ordinariness.

As practice deepens, the extraordinary hides inside the ordinary.

A breath.

A pause.

A moment of noticing.

We do not arrive anywhere.

Over time, we simply notice where we already are.

Light fades.

Breath continues.

And somehow, even now, we belong to this moment.

The world remains unfinished.

So do we.

And perhaps nothing more is needed here

This is quietly noticing

Here we are

Still.